MENTAL WEALTH

MENTAL WEALTH

5 HEALTHY PRINCIPLES TO WIN WITH MONEY

JEREMIAH REED

NEW DEGREE PRESS

MENTAL WEALTH

5 Healthy Principles to Win with Money

ISBN   978-1-64137-940-3 *Paperback*

978-1-64137-744-7 *Kindle Ebook*

978-1-64137-745-4 *Ebook*

If you wish to move mountains tomorrow,
you must start by lifting stones today.

AFRICAN PROVERB

*To my beautiful wife Selam and my children
Samiyah, Noah, and Yuel, without your sacrifice and
encouragement this book would not be possible.*

*May these words be written in your heart
and last forever in our family.*

CONTENTS

———

INTRODUCTION

"THE PROCESS"

Growing up, we learn that life lessons would come and go as we grew older. Our elders forgot to mention that the most important lessons come from failure, and not much is learned through success. In success, you learn what worked. You never have a chance to learn what does not work.

My life changed after an unforeseen event on a basketball court in 2016. It was the day before Father's Day, and I shattered my elbow playing basketball in Gary, Indiana. At that moment, I saw my future crumble before my eyes as I hit the concrete like a ton of bricks. It was the worst pain imaginable. The shock gave me a rush of adrenaline and courage. I was able to turn my chicken-winged arm back into a straight position. I realized my elbow was shattered, and I immediately started losing feeling in my right arm as it dangled like a wet noodle from a fork!

My arm was being held together by grace, and so was my financial life at that time. My hope for a speedy recovery and the grace of God was all I needed to pull through rehab. That sentence sounds simple, but there was a lot that went into pulling that off and fully using my arm again.

I had no short-term disability insurance to cover living expenses post-surgery, no extra money for rehab, no savings put aside for my family to live on while I was off work with a shattered elbow. I felt broken, both physically and financially. I have never told this story before because I felt ashamed. I kept it all hidden inside. I was afraid to let out how I truly felt.

The years following this accident would shape my life and help me start my debt-free journey. I had to break free and win the mental battle first. My moment of clarity came as I laid in that hospital bed. I was determined that I would never experience that level of brokenness again. I accepted God's plan for me.

The stress was at an all-time high during that time of my life. I now look back in amazement in comparison to where I am today. The debt had a powerful hold on my mind and behaviors.

My wife and I were $210, 711 in the hole when we began our road to prosperity. For the most part, I consider myself to be intelligent. I graduated first in my class in high school and graduated from the Kelley School of Business.

Numbers were not the issue.
It was my mindset.

My mental capacity to change my situation did not exist. I was numb to the truth of my decisions around money. The more I made, the more I spent. Even when I did not have it, I still spent it. If that isn't crazy, I don't know what it is.

Shattering my elbow was a blessing in disguise. At my lowest, I was able to gain mental clarity. My blinders were gone, and I was left to face my money monster. The steps I took to win with money were dependent on correcting my mindset towards money, by re-positioning my mind to the things that mattered most. I needed to affirm that money was not the end. It is the means to the end. Winning at money has nothing to do with the math we learn when we were in elementary school.

One of my favorite quotes is by Earl Nightingale in which he says,

"Don't concern yourself with the money. Be of service...build... work...dream...create! Do this and you'll find there is no limit to the prosperity and abundance that will come to you." [1]

The moment you realize your purpose is the moment everything else makes sense. Every day of our lives is a chance to change the old narratives about ourselves. A choice to go left or right, to stand up or sit down, to keep going or stop, and the list continues. Maybe you are buying this book because you feel that moment coming for you in your finances. Here is what you need to know about your answer.

---

1   Earl Nightingale, Earl Nightingale's Greatest Discovery: The Strangest Secret—Revisited (New York: Dodd, Mead, 1987).

Change your mindset, change your outcome. Live the life that was created for you by eliminating debt and allowing yourself to build real wealth.

Once you are debt-free, there is so much to look forward to and experience. Financial freedom is all about options. You can make decisions because you want to, not because you must. You deserve a financial situation that maintains your peace of mind. Paying off $210,711 in four years and ten months is not for a weary will. You are eternal, and your will does not get fatigued. The fatigue you feel is from the lack of abundance you have denied in your lifetime. Getting your financial life in order will allow the resources of financial wealth to flow through your life to bless you, your family, and those around you. It will take mental courage and self-discipline to get on track.

My prayer is this book will not only shift your mindset, but also teach you the principles to win the battle of the mind. Prosperity consciousness is necessary, and there are five Ps to help you gain confidence with money and destroy debt.

Purpose, Planning, People, Persistence, and Prayer are the key elements you need to build a money mindset. The key to keeping you moving through the process is passion—the feeling you get in your heart when you say you love something. This method follows the eighty/twenty principle.[2]

---

2   Dave Ramsey, "What's the Reason for the Debt Snowball—Ask Dave," daveramsey.com. 2020, https://www.daveramsey.com/askdave/budgeting/whats-the-reason-for-the-debt-snowball.

Personal finance guru Dave Ramsey once said,

"This is not a math problem; this is a behavior problem. Personal finance is 80 percent behavior and 20 percent head knowledge." [3]

Your probability of becoming wealthy has more to do with your response than it does your sophistication or your academic underpinnings.

Dave Ramsey was on to something, but nobody adequately addresses it. A lot of how-to books are based around the math side of things, but no one digs into the behavior side of things with real help for your mental health. Research in financial planning has demonstrated that advisers spend 25 percent of their time dealing with non-economic issues. Shockingly, the study also stated 74.4 percent had clients cry, sob, tremble, or become violent. Financial therapy is a new concept to help clients become more equipped to handle these situations, but is that enough?

Your mind is a tool that God gave you to do great things. The bad thing is we can be negatively influenced and broken by past money experiences. There were nights I could not sleep, but I was tired. I was tired of being sick to my stomach about all the money I owed people. Those sleepless nights allowed me to be real with myself. I had to admit that I needed help. I knew I was one crisis away from losing it all. I also knew there had to be something greater out there for me.

---

3   Ibid.

As I laid wake at night two questions kept pinging around my mind like unread email messages. "How do I change my behaviors with money?" I knew what was right, but I did the opposite.

The second was, "How do I stay fully engaged to complete such a mammoth task?" I admitted early on that I lacked motivation.

Brendon Burchard wrote in *The Motivation Manifesto,*

"We must remember we are not the sum of our intentions but of our actions."

Most people intend to be successful; it is those who take the actions toward success that arrive at their destination.

That is when God gave me the five Ps. My journey was not perfect, and I did not do all the right things all the time. However, I crossed the finish line, and now I want to help you do it. These five Ps mixed with passion helped serve as a guiding principle toward financial freedom.

Five Ps into Action

- **Purpose: Purpose** sets the end-goal and requires self-discipline. When you know what to do, you know what not to do.

- **Plans:** You need a **plan.** The Bible says a man makes his plans, but the Lord orders the steps. You must go beyond the budgeting and emergency funds. Ask yourself where you are going. How will I use the money to help others and change my family? The journey to financial freedom is not a stable walk uphill. It is like climbing a mountain. You will go up, back down, rest, back up, and probably back down. You will look out and see that even though the rough terrain, you are further along. You will build your financial stamina along the way. You need to learn how to handle burnout and hiccups along the way.

- **Persistence: Persistence** to finish. It takes will and consistency to move forward when others would stand still or retreat.

- **People:** An essential area of your journey and most significant impact on your mental health are the **people** you allow in your life. Whoever you choose to share your life with will impact you negatively or positively. Positive energy can lift you when you are down. Making sure you create and maintain a positive inner circle is vital.

- **Prayer: Prayer** also became my secret weapon. Staying in tune with God motivated me to keep going and kept my mind at peace. There were setbacks, but I looked at them as setups because I had been talking with God.

These five Ps do not mean anything if you are not passionate about winning with money.

Envision yourself on the other side of debt. Being a great steward empowers you to make decisions for you and your family because you are not confined by the small amount of money in your wallet. Dreams get bigger, but they also become a reality. If those thoughts do not move you enough to change, then your passion may be paralyzed by fear. That fear is related to success and your self-worth.

Do you think that you are not worthy enough to be financially free?

Prioritizing your mental health involving money is driven by believing you can do it. This is the Mental Wealth mindset for financial success. Get ready to improve your money mindset and destroy debt. Your mindset is the answer, not a bigger paycheck. I have learned a lot through my challenges of striving for financial freedom, and I cannot wait to share it with you.

Here are some expectations you might have with this book:
- You do not know where to start, or when you do start you expect quick results.
- You might have the expectation to be inspired to change your money habits.
- You might have hope of learning more about the five principles to apply it to other areas of your life.

Whatever your reason is, it is my prayer that this book blesses you with more abundance and help you live a more fruitful life with meaning. Being debt free is the first step in gaining control of your life and winning with money.

Please take notes, dig deep into your spirit, and venture to grow yourself. Being average is being broke.

Financing a $40,000 car when you make $40,000 a year before taxes is outrageous.

Spending without a budget is financial suicide.

Keeping up with the Joneses is unfulfilling.

I want you to enjoy money without stress, depression, and anxiety. You can begin to do it now. Get a pen and notepad ready. As you navigate through the pages of this book, write down things you have already started to do, and write down what you are prepared to add to your life. Remember this is a walk up the mountain, and not a race on straight flat surface.

Mental Wealth requires effort and dedication to achieve financial freedom.

CHAPTER 1

THE PROBLEM

―――

Money is not the green promissory note with dead presidents on it that stresses you. The experiences you have around money cause stress.

How well do you manage stress, and how often do you experience stress? This is a time to start looking at what triggers your stress. Waking up to multiple overdraft fees and waking up to a higher than expected bank balance causes two different reactions. Let me get you used to the feeling of having a consistently high bank balance!

If stress were a seed, it would be the most resilient plant to grow in the garden of your mind. Stress is a weed in the garden of God's temple. Your mind represents all potential varieties of flowers, plants, fruits, and vegetables. You are here to plant and harvest for as long as you walk this earth. Stress often hides in the shadows and grows wildly in those dark areas of negativity.

Begin to illuminate your mind with all God has promised me, you, and all humanity: plans to prosper and give us an expected end!

I interviewed several people before writing this book, and there was one common phrase that stood out: "I'm stressed out; I need financial help." A lot of people told me they tried Dave Ramsey, YouTube, and listening to podcasts like the Financial Grownup, but something was missing. Their stress and depression were still at an all-time high.

I recall one meeting I had with a client named Jennifer. She was the first person in her family to make it to college, and she racked up a lot of student loan debt out of ignorance. Like most of us, Jennifer did not have a smart plan to get in and out of debt. Her breaking point was not being engulfed by debt. What stressed her out most was she took on her family's financial problems because she was the savior of the family. Her family believed because she finished school and landed a great job that she could support them.

Jennifer owed that to her family right? Especially since her mom was first generation.

Wrong!

You can probably relate to Jennifer—are you the go-to person in your family?

You probably help cover utility bills, food, rent, car payments, and whatever else a family member might need.

You are the rainy-day fund!

You want to say no, but you cannot because you would feel selfish. These people helped you when you were younger, and now you owe them for life.

Stop it!

This savior complex will kill your mindset toward money. Running your financial home into the ground is seen as virtuous—only to level out and be right beside the people you bartered away your prosperity to help. Jennifer ended up $78,000 in debt and utterly depressed because she feels that she has nothing to show for all the hard work she puts in every week from 9 a.m. to 5 p.m.

Depression caused Jennifer to not eat, lose sleep, and push friends away out of resentment. When I asked Jennifer what her financial mindset was, she was a deer in headlights. I told her, "Choose to have a poverty mindset or an abundance mindset." Her thoughts would guide every decision she made from now on.

A positive mindset is hardly mentioned outside of academics when it comes to money. However, research suggests this relationship deserves the spotlight. According to an article by the Journal of Mental Health, money, finances, and debt are the most common source of anxiety. Forty-four percent of Americans report stress due to money issues.

Reading this caused me to dig deeper and analyze my own life. The truth is financial issues bring a lot of tension to people because of the focus we have on money in our society today.

Consider this: if you cannot pay your rent, you will be homeless. Miss enough car payments, and your car will be repossessed. The fear of what happens when money is mismanaged is enough to make the hairs on the back of your neck stand up before you ever sign your line to a contract. We must deal with the psychological effects behind money in order to win with money.

Feelings and thoughts are closely related to each other. Your feelings are sensations that are formed into your thoughts. Feelings of sadness, depression, and anxiety, if left unchecked, will develop into suicidal thoughts—a scary thing when it is all based on the negative responses you have toward mismanaging your money. This type of mindset is the opposite of having a positive financial mindset.

In the midst of the global pandemic, the US Bureau of Labor Statistics reported America has seen thirty-three million people file for employment between the end of March and beginning of May due to companies shutting down operations to stop the spread of the virus.

Thirty-three million individual's financial situations flipped upside down in a matter of months. Some of you reading this might have been impacted. My heart goes out to you if you were financially or physically impacted by COVID-19.

Those numbers are heartbreaking. Taking your finances more seriously and getting everyone around you on board is essential. A shift in wealth is occurring, and I want to see you and your family in foreign lands enjoying the life of financial security. Most financial advisers will not solve mindset issues; they deal with only financial matters. The relationship between poor mental mindsets and economic troubles is a continuous cycle that everyone needs to break.

Making a significant financial decision is hard when you are under stress and with a negative attitude. Being under pressure is a normal part of life, but if you are often overwhelmed by stress, these feelings are not healthy and can be counterproductive in any stage in life, especially the milestones.

When I was $210,711 in debt, I often hid my feelings. I wouldn't share how I was feeling inside, but I responded in ways that covered up my reality. I tried to purchase items to bring me happiness, but you can't find joy in items. The Jordan sneakers will get old, the jewelry might lose that extra sparkle, and there will always be a new something to come out that catches your attention.

You can't buy your way to financial freedom and peace—it is not for sale.

I took the wrong approach in the beginning because my mindset was defeated. I finally broke this cycle when I began to take healthy steps to take care of my mind by focusing on rewiring how I thought about things. Restoration is what happened to me. New seeds of thought were planted one at a time to form financial clarity.

CONNECTING THE DOTS

Your thoughts shape your reality; if you believe you are broke, you will always be broke. If you let money become your master, it will bring you to fear, and it will rule over you. You are behaving like a grasshopper, and you are here to overcome the giants in this land. Money is a giant to most of us and a servant of opulence to others. Your relations with money have trapped you in a maze, and fear is a blindfold. Having a healthy mind is an asset that keeps on paying dividends each day. You can navigate the maze with or without the blindfold and still finish the maze.

Mental Wealth is my solution for creating healthy habits and to fix your relationship with money. Mental Wealth is an all-inclusive mindset approach to help you win with money by focusing on your Purpose, Plan, People, Persistence, and Prayer to get you to financial freedom. Mental Wealth is the beginning of understanding who you are, where you need to go, and how you will get there. The truth is we all need to embrace healthy mindsets as we pursue financial security.

Your poor financial decisions can cost you more than owning a home or interest. It can cost you your life. According to the National Institute of Mental Health, one in five US adults experience a mental illness. Further research found mental health issues are three times higher among people who have debt. Depression, anxiety disorders, and psychotic disorders were among the most common mental illnesses experienced by people in debt.

Paying off debt was not a result of luck, it was a result of throwing away the old mindset money and awakening to a new one.

Paying off debt is a life-freeing experience that improves your mental health and sets up your children for a head start in life once you get a hold of your money issues.

Besides the psychological problems that come from poor financial decisions, you are also more likely to experience drinking problems and drug dependence. Creditfix published an article in 2017 titled "Alcohol and Debt—What are the Problems and Effects." [4] In this article, they stated, "The depressant effect which alcohol has on the brain generally results in a poorer judgment, causing a person to act impulsively and make decisions they would not normally make."

This experience makes you prone to money purchasing mistakes. You can no longer continue to wash your troubles down with a shot of bourbon and a Coke chaser. You also cannot smoke cannabis and watch your debt float away. These habits come from how you deal with stress.

The financial problem you face has a better answer, and it is entirely achievable with the right mindset. The result of your success is quite high when you shift to an infinite mindset. Simon Sinek wrote a book called The Infinite Game.[5] In it, he mentioned, "We do not think in quarters," he says, "we think

---

4   "Alcohol and Debt—What Are the Problems & Effects," Creditfix,
     August 15, 2017.
5   —. 2019. The Infinite Game. Portfolio/Penguin.

in generations." [6] Paying off debt is a finite concept. In the game of life, that is just a small part. The decisions you make are not just for you; it's for everyone around you, your children to come, and the strangers you will impact throughout your life. An infinite mindset is not a new idea; it was initially introduced by Professor James P. Carse. He is the author of Finite and Infinite Games: A Vision of Life as Play and Possibilities.[7]

Carse stated that winning and losing stemmed from a finite game, and thinking like this could be detrimental in an infinite game. Your financial well-being is not just about winning and losing, it is also about sustainability. Your wealth must live beyond your death.

Imagine if billionaire Robert Smith was pinching pennies and living check to check, and never feeling good enough to make something of himself. Imagine what The Morehouse Class of 2019 commencement speech would have been like without him. Would it have become a viral celebration of philanthropy? Probably not, and overall the life of the three hundred ninety-six college graduates would be vastly different.[8] This same imaginary concept holds true for you—do not leave anything on the table. Make sure this world experiences everything you have to offer.

---

6   Simon Sinek.*Start with The Why.*Portfolio; Reprint edition (December 27, 2011).

7   James P Carse, *Finite and Infinite Games: A Vision of Life as Play and Possibility.* New York: Free Press, n.d.

8   "Robert F. Smith's Morehouse Student Loan Pledge Will Also Include Graduate's Parents," BET.com, September 20, 2019, https://www.bet.com/news/national/2019/09/20/robert-f--smith_s-morehouse-student-loan-pledge-will-also-includ.html.

THE ANSWER: MENTAL WEALTH

Mental Wealth is more than a book title, it's a five-step principle-based process. This mindset change leads to a lifestyle change that produces positive financial results. The change is designed to get the thoughts of scarcity and poverty aligned with abundance and prosperity. Paying off debt for me was just the beginning of my financial journey, not the end. Mental Wealth goes beyond eliminating debt; it is about teaching you to rewire your mind, change your relationship with money, and build real wealth! Purpose, Planning, People, Persistence, and Prayer are principles that will be applied to your new life.

Wealth is more than money. Wealth is a universal term that covers health, time, relationships, and finances. This book will stick with the financial department, but what you will learn will also spill over into the other buckets, so take advantage of this new mindset.

Five principles guide this process; each principle represents the mindset you need to have. The principles are Purpose, Planning, People, Persistence, and Prayer. The glue that holds this together is your Passion. Passion is the effort you put in to make everything else work. You cannot have financial freedom without mastering the five principles.

1. Purpose is a mindset that helps put everything into proper perspective. It gives you your "why" and enables you to create a vision of your future. Purpose is the foundation of Mental Wealth, and without it, Mental Wealth has no meaning.

2. Planning is an action, but I want to teach you a new mindset to have toward it. Everyone makes plans, but little follow through with them. A plan is a finite thing, but you can make it infinite when you combine it with a long-term approach for your financial journey.

3. People are a unique component. We forget people play a crucial role in our financial journey when planning. You are the sum of the people around you. Choosing the wrong people will mentally stress you and even set you back. Identifying who lifts you up and who brings you down takes time, but can be achieved. Mental Wealth creates awareness in this category to support your financial well-being.

4. Persistence is all about mental grit. Facing the truth about who you are and being open to growth is the key. Nurturing that inner person will help you to remain steadfast on your journey. Listen to your thoughts and act. You already know what failure looks like, but what does victory look like for you? The dream is worth it; your vision is worth it. Some people grow tired, but ask yourself: what will separate you from everyone else? The answer is persistence.

5. Prayer is the most powerful principle. It is a chance for you to recharge, gain clarity, and gain strength. Prayer is my secret weapon. It allows me to put away what the world is telling me is possible for me. Prayer allows God to speak directly to my heart and tell me what he can do for me.

Mental Wealth principles are tools to change your life and set you on a path to win and master your finances for generations to come. A healthy mindset is your greatest asset.

Say goodbye to old ways and the old you. It is now time to say hello to your new life.

American author and former staff writer for The New York Times, Harold "Hal" Glen Borland, said it best. "No winter lasts forever; no spring skips its turn." [9]

The seasons we face in our life determine the rate of growth in our life. The significant part is that no season is permanent. Seasons in life provide a chance to plant, germinate, grow, and rest. Reflect on a season in your life where nothing was going well. Now think about a season where you seemed to lose track of time. The truth is we all experience these ups and downs. Money is no different. Are you aware of the term rainy days? There had to be a sunny day to prepare for a "rainy day." Do not get caught up in your rainy days. Better days will come, and you must be prepared for them when they do.

A healthy mindset will help you prepare for every season you encounter. The more you train your mind and practice positive mental habits in the five areas I addressed, the better your outcome will be when it comes to money. You are going from surviving to thriving; this is a beautiful time for you.

---

9   BrainyMedia Inc. "Hal Borland Quotes." Accessed May 30, 2020. https://www.brainyquote.com/quotes/hal_borland_143123.

CHAPTER 2

PURPOSE

—

MY LOVE STORY

November 29th in 2014 was a cold day. I had just worked a double at Macy's since it was Black Friday, but I was not sleepy. I was full of energy, and I could not get my future wife off my mind. It was one of my milestones; it was the day I said I do. There was some anxiety, but I was filled mostly with excitement. It felt like a championship game, and the ball was in my hands. I blocked all the naysayers and focused on one thing, the love I had for Selam. We were both young, in our early twenties, full of love and missing some direction. I told myself to let us get married first, and I would figure the rest out. There were no conversations about debt. We never discussed how we felt about loaning our money to others, merging our accounts, or what we wanted for our future. We were just two love birds without a clue.

November 29th ended, and well, that is when reality set in. That was when we had our first money fight. I am not going to say who started it. My wife would kill me, but let's just say merging accounts without a clear expectation is a bad idea! The conversation went like this: "Hey, why do we have a bill of $1500? I do not recall making any large purchases." You can imagine how the rest of the conversation went. We are only human. Feel free to insert what happens when you argue with someone. That credit charge was our first step down the hill of debt. It was a loan taken out for a family member—$1500 gone—and added to our liability category.

Well, there was something else that added to our growing debt as a couple. My wife financed a beautiful new 2014 Honda Civic for graduation. The salesman even convinced my wife that tire insurance was vital, and he rolled that tire package into the car and financed that as well! A $1,200 tire warranty would turn into $1,379.47. Let's not stop there, because I felt entitled and got a brand new 2013 black Nissan Altima—a gift to myself for graduation. I fell for the "new graduate program" discount. Our life just started, and we were paying $357 per month for my car and $423 for my wife's car. The $36,000 in student loans did not hit yet, and we were only making minimum payments on everything else.

We were the epitome of looking good, but dead broke.

We were asleep and living the "American Dream," somebody had to wake us up! We managed to make more poor financial decisions as time went on. Macy's got much of my paycheck because of how much I spent there throughout the week. We even financed our twelve-inch memory foam bed. Yep, every night was sleeping in debt and on debt.

I was the average American college graduate with real problems and a new wife. Please believe me when I say, paying off $210,711 took hard work! I made a lot of sacrifices, but I had to become crystal clear on my purpose. I had to create a plan for my family and myself.

I hit a wall, and my season came. I knew enough was enough. In that season, I realized I worked way too hard not to have anything to show for it. I was in the middle of winter in 2015.

Winters are cold and sometimes brutal. I grew up near Chicago, and the kiss of a winter breeze was nothing to take lightly. The windchill alone could cause your body to freeze. That unfavorable weather taught you how to plan. I spent most of that winter in self-reflection and meditation on where I went wrong. I was a smart guy; I graduated first from East Chicago Central. I went on to graduate from one of the top business schools in the country, the Kelley School of Business, but I was still a financial failure early on in my life.

I felt that I had the plan to change, and nothing was going to stop me. My wife supported this new attitude, and the first signs of spring began. I was becoming the morning sun that shined on beds of snow that had settled over my life. I had grown from the darkness of victimhood and became driven to clear my debt as soon as possible. Winter days allow you to take shelter and reflect on what is going on in your life. Most people are not excited to run around when it is negative ten degrees outside. In negative-degree weather you must clean the snow off the car, warm the car up, and layer up just to go out. So, if you are like me you would rather just stay indoors and relax.

Winter was coming to an end. February 2015 was different. I was missing something. I knew that I needed to be financially free, but I lacked direction. Then God revealed his wisdom. I had no vision. While most people were looking forward to Valentine's Day, that year I was focusing on defining my financial vision for my family. Being debt-free and living an abundant life had consumed me, and I became obligated to my family and God to do so.

PUTTING THE PIECES TOGETHER
My Purpose

"First learn and then teach others how to manage money."

My Vision

"Innovate how people view managing money and build a financial legacy of stewardship for future generations."

My Mission

"Share the knowledge of money management across the world to create better financial stewards in every season of their life."

CHANGE OF HEART AND A RENEWED MIND
Let's get an official definition from Lexico.com to give us the explanation of purpose. That takes the pressure off this profound concept of purpose.

Purpose as a noun has two definitions.

The first definition is "the reason for which something is done or created or for which something exists." The second definition is "a person's sense of resolve or determination." Purpose as a verb or action is defined as "having as one's intention or objective."

I had to have a crystal-clear mindset to establish objectives for myself and my family. Through my years of observation and personal failures, I learned we can become professional beginners. Never finishing what we set our mind to do—I did not want that to be us. One area of focus to help you complete what you set out to do, is knowing your purpose, knowing the why behind your what.

In the book Start With Why, Simon Sinek stated there are

"Two ways to influence human behavior, you can manipulate it or inspire it." [10]

Your purpose must inspire you to pursue your financial goals at all costs. Having a clear purpose will help you stay true to your goal when times get hard. Your vision should drive you to self-discipline, which means self-imposed boundaries that prevent you from detouring from the goal you set for yourself to reach.

Simon has a concept called the Golden Circle. This concept correlates to finding your purpose on your journey toward financial freedom. The Golden Circle is based on starting with

---

10   Simon Sinek.*Start with The Why.*Portfolio; Reprint edition (December 27, 2011).

the WHY, then the HOW, and lastly with the WHAT. He goes on to explain that the limbic brain is a powerful piece of your body that creates strong emotions. These emotions turn into behaviors that drive you to accomplishing great things.

You need to know you WHY when you set your financial goals, tackle debt, or sit down to plan for your future. Your WHY is the fuel that will keep your motor running during the journey.

The financial vision I created that February consisted of two simple concepts.

1. To master the resources given to me: "become a better steward of what I already have."
2. God's will, for me, is to live a life of abundance in every area of my life.

I was not looking to complicate life. I wanted the vision to be clear and stand for something my wife could rally behind. Vision is about where you see yourself going. Sometimes vision cannot be seen by the eyes but can be expressed in the imagination.

I saw myself debt-free, blessing others, and a legacy that would enrich my loved ones and others forever.

No one can walk, train, or complete our journey for us. We must embrace our uniqueness and find our WHY. I was tired of not having enough, afraid of what could happen next, and, most of all, wasting my seasons of wealth. You cannot work forever, so you must get smart with the income you earn today. Do you have a vision, and what is your WHY?

I want to explore this with you and help you frame this out. Without defining your financial vision, the rest of this book means nothing. Trust me, you will be more likely to quit without a vision.

Excuses will come, and they sound like, "no one will help me," "the government is holding me down," "Uncle Sam is taking too much," "I must help others before myself," and "life is just too hard." Do not entertain these types of thoughts. No matter the excuse, know that God can deliver his grace through any person, place, or thing. God will make way for you if you make it clear of what your intentions for your life are.

There is power in knowing your purpose and having a vision. For example, let's study the marathon runner named Ryan Hall. Ryan is a retired American long-distance runner who went to Stanford University and held the US record in the half marathon at fifty-nine minutes and forty-three seconds. He is the only American to run under 2:05 for a marathon.

With all these accolades, you would think he grew up loving to run. You would think Ryan had the best body and always stayed in tip-top shape and never had any self-doubt. Do you know where I am going with this? It was the complete opposite. Ryan shared his story on an episode of EntreLeadership entitled "Run the Mile You're In." [11]

---

11   Ryan Hall, The EntreLeadership Podcast Episode 336: Run the Mile You Are In, interview by Alex Judd, August 18, 2019.

It started when he was thirteen. Like most teenage boys, he tried a few sports, baseball, basketball, and football, but nothing seemed to have a promising future for him. However, he pushed himself because he was not a quitter. He stated,

"he remembers looking out over a lake, and God planted this burning desire, that almost seemed outside himself to run around the lake."

This was no ordinary desire. The circumference of that lake was about fifteen miles. He ended up telling his dad about this enormous goal, and his dad said, okay, let's do it.

Guess what? He accomplished it!

He did not love it, but he made it. Getting out of debt was freeing, but I did not love every part of it. Like Ryan, I had roadblocks come up in life like family issues, car accidents, and employment changes. You must keep moving forward. Runners keep their heads up in a race to see where they are going. We must do the same. We must run the mile that we are in.

After a fifteen-mile run, Ryan remembered collapsing on the couch and having the spark of intuition from God. "I have given you a gift to run with the best guys in the world, but I gave you this gift so that you would help others." Ryan knew that was the moment everything changed for him. Ryan knew his purpose. He believed it was his destiny to go to the Olympics to run in the game and run with the best guys in the world. Ryan spent the next twenty years going after that vision. He was thirteen when he had this vision. Vision does not have an age bias.

Remember, you are never too young, and you are never too old to become receptive to your vision.

When a runner starts training, he or she is preparing their bodies and mind to finish the race. Ryan was not ready for the Olympics at the age of thirteen; he had to adjust. Runners do not just run, they are running with a purpose with an end goal in mind. That purpose might be to prove others wrong, beat a personal challenge, or for the love of the race. Like a runner, your motive will turn into your fuel when doubt, fear, or lack of discipline creep up on you. Therefore, you must know your "why," and it should be the reason you are ready to get out of bed every morning. Going against society is hard when it comes to managing your money and living on less than you make; that is why your purpose and vision are the two most critical components to becoming debt-free.

On my journey to financial freedom, I found myself driving back to my "why" often. Dr. Myles Munroe was a Bahamian minister, speaker, and leadership consultant. Dr. Munroe died in a devastating plane crash on November 9th, 2014. He was known for his wisdom, and during a conference, he stated:

"purpose is your ultimate original reason for creating a thing." [12]

I refused to continue to live paycheck to paycheck and squander away my resources. One of my driving forces was to be debt-free was solely based on me being tired of being a bad steward of money. I needed to become better at managing

---

12   Myles Munroe. "Dr Myles Munroe | The Purpose for Your Life." Video, 32:39, https://youtu.be/EJ7Xz_mLsN4.

my resources. Achieving this goal would open doors for me to help my family, heal my fear-based living, and, most of all, honor God.

Once I understood my purpose, I was able to define my vision. Visions are extraordinary, and they are unique to us; they are distinctive and alluring. It is a fully customized plan to fulfillment from God. You must bring your purpose to life! Vision is that guiding force that will keep you going onward, while others tell you to take a detour. You will know where you have been, where you're going, and how to get there.

Here is a short mental exercise to follow. Let us say you have a purpose related to transportation. You believe everyone should be able to get from point A to point B without walking. You discover that your mission in life is to create the world's best bus line. Let us go through how steps are created and what challenges do you face by answering these questions.

- How big is a single passenger bus?
- How will you get to the patrons?
- How much will you charge?
- Where will you start?
- When do you want this to be completed?

The answers to these questions will guide all your decisions and form your vision. Not knowing the answers to these questions will get you one step closer to not finishing what you started. Remember, once you have the vision, you can begin effectively working on the plan to resolve the challenges. Vision gives you the framework to help you accomplish what you desire. Once you achieve what you desire, you will see it reflected in your world; every realized desire becomes steps on the mountain to purpose.

Here is a real-life example of what happens when you do not have a vision but find changes in your life. I recently listened to the first episode of Borrowed Future, which is a brand-new podcast from Ramsey personality Anthony O'Neal. He is the author of "Debt-Free Degree." In this episode, he shared a remarkable story that resonated with me.

Anthony stated he had received a National Forensics League scholarship and G.I. Bill scholarship going into college, but he still made financial mistakes. He stated, "I still borrowed money to go after the lifestyle, to get the clothes, to get the car, to buy the roses, to go to McDonald's. I borrowed money just for the freaking lifestyle." [13] Those were his exact words. He spent his money on cars, clothes, and food.

He took out $10,000 in student loans. He spent $15,000 in credit cards and charged up to $10,000 on furniture. Anthony was nineteen and racked up $35,000 in debt. That led to him being homeless and sleeping in a car at the age of nineteen. He shared research which showed that the average college debt for a college graduate was around $32,000. And he was tired of being average.

That was his wake-up call. The solution to the problem was simple. Anthony stated, "I never took the time to write out a vision for me, there was no plan for my life. I just followed

---

13   Anthony O'Neal, "The Borrowed Future Podcast What No One Told You About Student Loans."

what everyone called normal—normal ended me up in the backseat of a car." [14]

What is blocking you from creating your vision? Without a vision to define his path, Anthony made foolish decisions. Nothing was set in place to guide him. We have all been there. I financed things I could not afford. I brought clothes to impress others, cars, rims, and gadgets.

These things are not bad; they were not right for me at that moment because I could not afford them.

I lacked that same vision as Anthony. I financed my bed because I wanted a memory foam bed when it first came out! Can you believe that? I was following the status quo. Instant gratification drove all my decisions, and that lead me to being $210,711 in debt. The payoff of instant gratification kept me in bondage; I was tethered to the things I thought I could not live without.

I am pleased to hear Anthony found his vision and his purpose in his darkest season. Now he is a thought leader on how to go to college debt-free. In our country, student loan debt is climbing beyond $1.6 trillion. That number just makes my stomach twist like a New York-style pretzel, hold the mustard, light on the salt. There is no such thing as winning in

---

14 Daveramsey.com. "What No One Told You About Student Loans." accessed June 08. 2020. https://www.daveramsey.com/blog/what-no-one-told-you-about-student-loans.

the money game if you owe someone everything you have. No one would listen to me about managing money if...

I was living paycheck to paycheck.

My children had no savings for college.

I could not afford a simple $500 emergency.

The list goes on. I had to help myself before I could teach others how to turn around their financial situation. This vision became my driving force to beat debt and honor God in my finances.

Vision is the insight of intuition. Vision gives meaning to the purpose. So, ask yourself, what is your purpose? Do you know what drives you? Why do you want to get out of debt, manage your money better, or simply win with money? If you are struggling to discover this, you are not alone.

However, I am here to help you figure this out. What if I told you it is a simple strategy?

To get to the heart of finding your purpose, here are three simple questions to get your brain and heart on the same page. You won't find a better person to listen to for help than Ken Coleman.

Ken Coleman is the father and author of the "Proximity Principle," a concept that he believes—and has proven—works. This principle will help you get to where you want to go and be who you want to be in life. For example, if you wish to coach basketball, you must find a way to get into the proximity of other coaches to learn, grow, and ultimately get to be a basketball coach. Ken is also the host of the Ken Coleman Show, where he gives people fresh career advice to help them land their dream job. Ken has set out on his mission to help as many people as possible find their purpose in their careers. He does it by observing people's "sweet spot." Your "sweet spot" is where your talents and passions meet.

Answer these three questions about yourself to find your "sweet spot."

Question 1
- What are you passionate about when you think about your financial future?
  -
  -
  -

Question 2
- Where are you naturally gifted when it comes to earning money?
  -
  -
  -

Question 3
- What pushes you when you want to give up, but you do not?
  -
  -
  -

Answering these questions honestly will help you define your purpose. If you do not know these answers yet, think about things that matter most to you, something you want to accomplish, and places you want to go. You can ask your friends and family these questions as well. They will most likely come up with the same observations about you. How much money do you need to accomplish these goals, and how vital is Godly stewardship to you? Vision is much simpler to define when you know your "why."

I define vision as the guiding pathway by which you make decisions that help you accomplish your purpose.

The Bible says in Proverbs 29:18, "Where there is no vision, the people perish, but he that keepeth the law happy is he." Vision in this context was also tied to God's purpose for humanity.

TESTING YOUR VISION

It was December 13th, 2016. It was snowing heavily in Indianapolis, Indiana. My wife and I were locked in on paying off our debt. We cleared off a little under $16,000 in 2015, and we had paid off a 2004 Honda Accord. I named her Silver Bullet. She was the perfect work car. My wife was a mobile recruiter, so she drove a lot of miles, and we thought getting something old would keep our insurance low. We were smart; life was going as planned; we were following the Dave Ramsey plan and had our emergency fund of $1,000 in place. Life was not perfect for us, but our vision kept us going.

The snow was not going to keep us from going to work. As usual, we gave each other our goodbye kisses, and "I love yous" before going our separate ways. We did not say a prayer that day for safety, but thanked God for guardian angels. They meet our needs even when we do not know them. Little did we know that this day would change our lives forever.

On my way to work, I was sliding on slick roads, but I just slowed down and paid attention to the road. I am from East Chicago, so navigating terrible weather conditions is standard. I had my wife on my mind the entire way to work. Perhaps I should have called her, but I wanted to let her focus on the road. She had to drive to Muncie, Indiana that morning.

After an hour passed, I received a phone call from my wife. Everything was inaudible; all I could hear was screaming and sobbing. I was instantly filled with fear and sadness.

I yelled back, what is wrong!

Where are you?

Are you okay?

I could hear the sirens and her crying. My wife finally responded, "I lost control" in a broken voice. I was convinced my wife had been hurt in an accident. I assumed the worst now and imagined her injured or crippled when I arrived. In my mind, nothing else mattered in that moment, not the debt, not the jobs we had, not anything.

In a blink of an eye, everything around you can change. So, forgive often and love with all your heart. You never know when the last chance was indeed the last.

My vision was being tested at this moment. How would I respond?

It took me an hour and a half to get to the crash site. My wife had been carried away in an ambulance. To my surprise, I got another phone call from my wife saying she was okay, and she wanted me to pick her up. I met the ambulance driver at the Loves gas station off I-69. I will never forget that moment I saw her. I squeezed her as tight as I could without hurting her bruised body. It was a miracle that she was still alive.

It was a four-car accident due to her sliding into oncoming traffic after hitting a patch of black ice. Silver Bullet took a beating. She was flipped over, hit from the back, and crushed on the side. All the airbags had deployed. When I went to the junkyard, I could not believe Selam had made it through it. I know God kept her alive for me, and I could never repay that debt.

The paid-off car totaled, $26,000 owed in subrogation due to not having enough coverage to pay off all the damage done to the other vehicles, and more hospital bills. The liability column was at an all-time high, but it was one thing in the win column that outweighed the losses.

Selam was alive!

My vision was on trial. I had to surrender. I had to verbalize and visualize myself at the finish line.

What did I really believe?

Would we be debt-free?

Could we overcome this loss?

How do we bounce back from this financially?

The questions ran rapidly through my mind as I interrogated myself. I took comfort in seeing my wife, and I was thankful I knew the formula to pull this together, it would just take more time. Your vision begins your journey, and no matter how dark a season could be for you, please keep going.

I would never wish a car accident on anyone; you never know what could happen in any season of your life. An emergency fund is great to have, but do not put your security in your savings. The $1,000 we had was nowhere near enough to cover what we were facing, but it was $1,000 cushion from the $26,000 blow that hit a hard reset on our financial progress. Dave's plan did not work for me.

I learned not to get caught up in the results and deadlines, but it is crucial to understand the "why" behind it. This is where your vision comes into place. You must know where you are going, especially when you face adversity. Winter seasons in your life do not always last. Snowstorms do cease. The sun comes out and melts the ice. The spring sun brings warmth to the winter season.

Write your vision below as a manifesto toward your new life toward financial freedom. Use a pencil so you can come back and make edits. Take your time and get this part right because winter has storms. Those storms will test the authenticity of your vision when the pressure is turned up and your back is against the wall.

CHAPTER 3

PLANNING

___

Are you ready to change?

Are you prepared t o stick to the plan you have set for yourself?

CNBC published an article on January 9, 2019, and it stated 78 percent of Americans live paycheck to paycheck.[15] This means they have no money to save and they are unable to cover an emergency. They are stuck in the rat race trying to survive. It is hard to look five to ten years down the road when your lights are off and you are hungry.

Most people try to solve the not enough money problem by increasing their income. The mindset states, "I have money problems, and more money will solve it." Increasing your money without addressing the root issues will later come back to haunt you. The Notorious B.I.G. had a song called "Mo' Money Mo' Problems."[16] This song outlined the

---

15   Emmie Martin, "The Government Shutdown Spotlights a Bigger Issue: 78% of US Workers Live Paycheck to Paycheck," *CNBC,* 2019.

16   The Notorious B.I.G, "The Notorious B.I.G. - Mo Money Mo Problems (Official Music Video)," YouTube Video, YouTube, 2020, https://www.youtube.com/watch?v=gUhRKVIjJtw.

premise of the mindset that money does not solve all problems. Do not neglect the psychology of the issues you're facing. Money issues have an emotional effect on you, and you must deal with these emotions.

Barton Goldsmith, PhD and licensed marriage and family therapist is an award-winning psychology writer. He is the author of seven books and is a columnist for both The Chicago Tribune and The Santa Barbara News-Press syndicated by Tribune Media. He wrote an article called "Money and Emotions," to encourage people that financial troubles are not the end of the world. [17] To control your emotions and fix your money issues there are some positive things that you can do.

You have heard of financial coaches and advisors jumping straight into the "B" word. No, I am not swearing, I am referring to the word everyone hates: BUDGET. Dr. Goldsmith stated that purchasing large items can build anxiety. When you do not know if you can afford an item, you begin to stress out over it and get anxious. One way to prevent this is to have a budget.

A budget is a self-imposed constraint you put on your spending habits in a specific category.

Budgets can be short term or long term. The most important thing you must understand about a budget is knowing what the

---

17   Barton Goldsmith, "Money & Emotions," *Psychology Today,* 2018.

numbers represent. Numbers tell stories, and those stories have a meaning. A budget lets us know what we can afford and what we cannot, which relieves a lot of stress when it comes to money.

When I was in debt, I sucked at budgeting. I consistently over-spent in the clothing department and food. My self-discipline was weak, and I told a lie to myself to keep me from reaching my goal. Every single time I missed the goal, I felt like a complete failure. Failure brought sadness and ultimately drained my energy from trying again. Then it clicked for me: budgets are finite. What if I made them infinite? What if life was all about tradeoffs? Failing to hit the budget in January was not so bad if you looked at your overall budget for the whole year.

EMBRACE IMPERFECTION

Your financial journey may have bumps in the road. There will be times you overspend, fail to plan for a significant expense, underestimate your ability to cover something, or drop the ball. Knowing that you are not perfect will prepare your mind to handle failure appropriately.

Say this out loud: it is okay to fail.

Just make sure you get back up. Coco Chanel stated,

"Success is most often achieved by those who don't know that failure is inevitable."

Coco began her life in an orphanage where she learned to sew. She made sewing her life's work. You may know her company as CHANEL.

For example, I always set a goal to work out more. I go a bit deeper and say I am going to do it three times a week for one hour. Guess what happens? After I have a week of only going to the gym once, I fall off. I feel like I failed myself, and I lack the motivation to try it again. Your budgets are no different. You set a monthly plan, quarterly, or evenly yearly budgets, and as soon as you blow one category, you fail the whole month. Have you ever asked yourself why you do that?

The "planning fallacy" is a term coined in 1979 by Daniel Kahneman and Amos Tversky. [18]

The planning fallacy means when you have a task, you are so optimistic that you underestimate what is truly needed to complete the task. I used to think, "We only have $80,000 in debt, we can eliminate that in two years." As you may know, that is not how my story ended up. Eighty thousand dollars turned into $210,711, and it took four years and ten months to pay that off.

When you are making your debt-free plans or savings plans, you must be careful to avoid falling into planning fallacy traps. Roger Buehler made it simple for us when he said "planning fallacy" is only every day, old wishful thinking. You are more than a wishful thinker, and you will become financially free. Please realize your journey is not expected to be perfect, and instead of staying down, get back up just one more time.

---

18   Roger Buehler and Dale Griffin, "The Planning Fallacy: Cognitive, Motivational, and Social Origins,"Advances in Experimental Social Psychology43. 2010.

BEATING WISHFUL THINKING

I came across an interesting article in M.D. Magazine called "How to Defeat Wishful Thinking."[19] The advice was practical, and I loved the perspective it came from. Most people know doctors make a lot of money, but have you ever considered the other half of the story? The average student loans for a doctor is around $206,000, according to Studentloanplanner.com.[20] Could you imagine paying $2,100 a month on a standard ten-year repayment option? Here are some safeguards to help you fight against wishful thinking and protect your mind from being damaged by false expectations. You can write these principles down in your financial freedom journal to help you stay engaged and motivated during your journey.

TIP 1—MAKE IT A CHALLENGE

If you willingly go into something knowing it will be difficult, it prepares you for the bumps and bruises. No one says climbing Mount Everest is easy. They prepare for that hike like their life depends on it (because it does). When you hear about a challenge, I want you to think of it as an opportunity to prove to yourself and others how great you are. Where there is no challenge, there is no growth. Becoming debt-free is not easy. Take the challenge on headfirst and enjoy the ride. Every turn, every bump, every hill, and every pit stop. Set benchmarks for yourself to track your progress. I reminded myself once a month that I was in a fight, and as that debt number kept dwindling, it was letting me know who was winning that battle.

---

19   "How to Defeat Wishful Thinking," HCPLive®, 2016.

20   Student Loan Planner, "Student Loan Planner - Student Loan Advisor and Expert," Student Loan Planner, August 8, 2019.

TIP 2—MAKE IT A COMPETITION

You might be reading this part and saying, "I am not a competitive person. I am an introvert. I hate keeping score." All those things are excuses. You just have not found something you are passionate about. If you genuinely want to get out of debt and live a full life independent of others, this friendly competition is just for you. Find someone who has similar goals and is heading on the same path you are on. I used my friend close to me to fuel my fight on debt. I mentally played a game on who would pay certain things off first or who could save up their emergency fund first.

Competition can be healthy for you, both emotionally and physically. It will help you stay focused and willing to keep plowing through when you want to quit. This is a healthy conflict to engage in during your financial walk. This nudge is excellent for fighting depression because you will get to see you are not alone in this battle, and the person you are going against is not your enemy. Both of you can achieve financial success at the end of the fight. Talk to someone close to you that you trust, and let the games begin.

TIP 3—MAKE IT A TREAT

Reward-based motivation is still one of the most dominant forms of motivation. This positive reinforcement works excellent if you are the person who mentally needs this kind of boost during your journey. Celebrate the small wins along the journey.

During the journey, my wife and I would reward ourselves with a movie and dinner. Nothing too big. Sometimes it would even just be a night of bowling. We used these little nights or evenings of fun to remind us what it would be like when we did not have other people to pay anymore.

Find the rewards that get you motivated. You do not have to go day to day, week to week, and month to month, dreading each moment of your journey. When you take care of business financially, treat yourself for it. Your mental health is especially important during your journey, so reward yourself when you hit a goal.

Meg Selig is the author ofChangepower! 37 Secrets to Habit Change Successand has been a blogger for about five years. She earned her MA Ed. in counseling at Washington University in St. Louis. In 2017, Meg wrote an article for Psychology Today titled "How Do Work Breaks Help your Brain? Five Surprising Answers." [21]

Meg discovered that taking breaks can help with decision fatigue. Author S.J. Scottpoints outthat the need to make frequent decisions throughout your day can wear down your willpower and reasoning ability. When you take a break, you can recharge your brain and make better decisions. A financial journey takes a lot of focus and determination. Failure to give your routine a pit stop can be poisonous.

My son Noah and I love to watch an animated movie called Cars. There was a scene where Lighting McQueen thought he could win the race without going in for a pit stop. He looked

---

21   Meg Selig, "How Do Work Breaks Help Your Brain? 5 Surprising Answers," *Psychology Today*, 2018.

to be on top for a while, but he realized the importance of a pit stop. His tire blew toward the end of the race and caused him to lose. Though this is funny to see for my two-year-old, this was sad because I have coached people and seen people blow right before the finish line in their financial lives.

Here are some practical things you can do to take a "break" and reward yourself on your financial journey to avoid burnout or decision fatigue.

- Get more rest!
- Give yourself permission to binge watch your favorite TV show
- Create a self-care day, DIY bath bombs, scrubs, and masks
- Take paid time off just to relax
- Look on Groupon and get a massage or a pedicure and manicure
- Exercise

Those are just a few things to reward yourself with for hitting your financial goals when trying to get out of debt. Do not forsake the power of a reward you care about. If you are in a relationship, you can even use this section to spice some things up.

BEATING DEADLINE STRESS

Besides wishful thinking, you also face the pressure of hitting deadlines you put on yourself regarding paying off debts or hitting your financial goals. These timelines add on extra stress when you miss them and could hinder you from pursuing other goals you set out to complete due to fear of failure.

Here is a solution to help you. This next part might sound like a cheat code, but it is vital during the planning stage of your process of hitting those deadlines: Cut the goal in half or double the time you give yourself to hit the goal. This takes the psychological pressure off you so you can relax and execute the plan.

CUT THE GOAL IN HALF

If you said, "I want to lose ten pounds this month," and you failed, how would you feel? You would feel mentally defeated. Now let us take that same goal and say, "I want to lose ten pounds in two months," and you ended up losing twelve pounds. How would you feel? Your mental state would be in a lot better place, and you would be motivated to continue working out.

I tried this method out while I was paying off debt. See, we're naturally inclined to chase perfection and to do it quickly. But paying off debt is more like a marathon than a race, so we cannot take race concepts and expect to win the marathon. I told myself I wanted to pay $1,000 a month on a PNC Bank account for four months until it was paid off. This goal sounded great to me until life hit. I had to reset my expectations to $500 a month. That was my new minimum. The goal was not the number per month; it was the result I was chasing. Paying off PNC was my end game; whether it is $500 a month or $1000, the job was just to get it done.

This small example could be put to work for whatever financial goal you have. This concept will give you grace, so when you miss that high expected number, you still are motivated to continue. Cutting a goal in half refocuses your mindset and fights against depression, anxiety, and stress. Do yourself a favor and cut the goal. You will be surprised at what will happen. Cutting things in half creates small victories for you to cheer for.

New York Times bestselling author Jon Acuff created "The 30 Days of Hustle Program." In his book entitled Finished, he discussed on the ninth day of the program that he told his participants to cut their goals in half, and "those who listened found 90 percent more desire to work on their goal. It encouraged them to keep going, and it motivated them to work harder because the goal seemed attainable."[22]

Jon was onto something. He also discovered during this program, 63 percent of the people who cut their goal in half saw increased performance. Take a sheet of paper and write down all your financial goals. It could save plans or paying off debts. See if you can cut the goal by doubling the time needed to hit the goal. Start with one goal and test this theory. It will bless you and improve your mental health.

DRUNK OFF OPTIMISM

I am a positive guy and believe in positive energy, but you must be cautious of too much optimism. The goal you set must be realistic to hit. Do not play the mental game of success with your mind. For example, let's hypothetically say you want to own an NBA franchise by the age of thirty, and you are currently twenty-eight. There are a plethora of

---

22   John Alcuff.Finish: *Give Yourself the Gift of Done*.Portfolio. 2017.

checkpoints you need to hit before reaching that goal. For starters, the average NBA team is worth $1.9 billion, according to Forbes. If your current net worth is less than twenty thousand, how would you expect to hit that goal in two years?

We sometimes overestimate our natural talents, and we drink the "Secret Stuff" from Space Jam.[23] I know you believe in yourself, and I know you will hit your goal, but you have done enough negative self-talk. I want you to avoid those pitfalls, so relax and follow the path of least resistance.

The saying "Rome was not built in a day" is right about a lot of things, and your debt-free financial journey is one of them. Be positive, but do not become drunk with optimism. Optimism has a strong influence on your mental health. There are plenty of researchers discussing how being positive helps your mental capacity, but just like anything else, too much is not always best.

OVERCOMING THE FIGHT OF THE BALANCING ACT

I am here to break some bad news to you about work-life balance. It's hard to accomplish, but it can be done.

Hitting your goals takes a lot of hard work. That work might consist of more time away from family or other key things you value.

There will be seasons where you need to work more or seasons when you need to be there for your family more. Choose a balance that is ideal for you. More hours at work means

---

23   Space Jam(Warner Bros. Pictures, 1996).

the debt getting paid off quicker, more time at home means finding ways to bond with family within your budget. You must learn how to make consistent deposits into your family, so even if you are not there, they still feel your presence!

A deposit is not a bank transaction for this purpose; it is not a quick exchange. A deposit is not something you do out of obligation. A deposit is an intentional relational act for a loved one. Being intentional is key. You must schedule that time for your loved ones. New York Times bestselling author Michael Hyatt said,

"If you want to master your schedule, increase your efficiency and output, and create more margin in your life for the things you care about, you've got to learn how to focus. When your focus is off, you will begin to be spread too thin."

When was the last time you deposited into yourself? If you cannot answer this, take a moment and schedule it soon.

Depression creeps in when you feel that you are spinning your wheels, and you are losing financially and relationally. I struggled with this, and I must admit my mental health took a hit. I was driving for Uber and Lyft, doing resumes, and working a full-time job. I was "busy." I felt like my relationship with my wife and children was terrible! I was depositing more money into my account, but at what expense? I was not focused because I was trying to be balanced.

During your journey, you get to choose when you work and when you deposit into your family. A date night goes a long way. A movie night with children or a coloring contest goes a long way. Figure out what your loved ones value and do it. There is no secret behind this principle—it is simply based on you being focused and intentional. Remember no one wins when it is fifty-fifty.

YOU CAN'T DO IT ALL

When you keep adding something to your plate, something will fall off. You cannot continue to juggle everything and expect to get everything done. Do not become a jack of all trades and master of none.

When you are trying to get out of debt, it becomes your number one priority.

You must remember your purpose and the vision you cast for yourself. There will be things you simply cannot do because it does not align with your goal of crossing that debt-free finish line. Preparing for this mentally upfront will save you a lot of stress.

Planning out what you are willing to drop the ball on helps you manage your stress and strengthens your ability to tell people no. Writing this book took a lot. I had to say no to my friends often when it came to social functions. I also decided to drop the ball on basketball. Your dropping will be unique to you and your journey. During my debt-free journey, my wife and I dropped the ball on a few essential things that hurt us a little bit emotionally, but knowing our "why" helped us conquer that mental battle.

We said no to the big "v" word: vacations. Seeing all the pictures on Instagram and Facebook was tough, but we made a promise to each other to clean up this mess at all costs. One of those costs were vacations. I missed my best friend's wedding in the Dominican Republic, not because we did not have the money, but because we decided to throw the money on debt. Those decisions are complex and are mentally draining. Your mental health is a vital component to making those decisions with a clear mind. It is easy to feel trapped by others and what they expect from you in these situations.

I think vacations were the easiest to let go of. I missed a lot of Jordan release dates. My wife thought it was mature of me, and she knew I did not need any more shoes, but that was hard. For years, I bought Jordans, and I collected over seventy-five pairs, but it was time to tackle debt. Unlike Jordan, I dropped the ball.

Dropping the ball might feel bad in the beginning, but it will feel even better for you in the end. When you knowingly drop the ball, you remove that shame and guilty feeling, which improves your mental mindset toward failing. The key is controlling what you choose to do and knowing why you did it.

It is your journey, and you should have fun. What is more potent than a SMART goal? A fun goal! People work harder when they are having fun! I asked several people who started a debt-free plan who quit shortly after starting. Why did they stop? The answers all had something in common. They were not having fun. We are all motivated by two things, fear, or rewards, and you can plug in fun to both categories.

Rewards should make this process fun. On my journey, I told myself for every $10,000 we paid off of our debt, I would get myself a new suit. I also rewarded my wife with special days to the nail salon. I never go in because I hate the smell, but I love how it makes her feel and how she looks, so it is a win for both of us. Channel that inner kid and simply have fun. Being in debt is stressful, and the last thing you need is more pressure.

Having fun with fear takes a person who is entirely in control of their mental health. In some ways, it is like psyching yourself out. Do you remember Fear Factor?[24] It was a TV show based on conquering your fear but in a fun way. The famous saying was, "fear is not a factor." How do you apply this to your money battles? It takes a little bit of creativity, but you can do it. I want you to think about everything you do not like. Things that just bug you. Write them all down. This will be called your budge list. Now let us attach dollar amounts to them.

For example, I hate bugs. I am going to challenge myself and say if I miss a $50 payment on my credit card, I will eat a cooked bug! That is disgusting. I want to puke just thinking about it. Then you find a crazy friend who will hold you accountable. I went left with that example to exaggerate the point, but I hope you get it. It is simple, just have fun. Fun releases dopamine and adrenaline to keep you moving forward and happy along the way.

According to Psychology Today, dopamine is the feel-good neurotransmitter—a chemical that ferries information between neurons. These imperative neurochemicals boost

---

24 Joe Rogan, "Fear Factor," n.d.

mood, motivation, and attention, and help regulate movement, learning, and emotional responses. Enjoying the process but disliking the day is okay; however, enjoy your journey. Have fun when you plan to succeed, and if you fail. Here is something I created called the Ideal Budget to help you have a foundation for building a plan to help you spend your money wisely.

The mindset behind planning fun is to go beyond the numbers. It is a mental tool that helps you maintain your mental health. You're going to need to have fun on your way to financial freedom.

THE IMPORTANCE OF A BUDGET

The journey to financial freedom is about hitting your goals. Getting out of debt, saving for retirement, and saving for a vacation are all goals. No matter the goal, the strategy is the same. You must have a plan and your mental health matters every step of the way. Figuring this out was a game-changer for my family. We crushed our debt because we were able to turn our plan into goals. Budgets and numbers will always be there, and they are essential; however, you cannot forget to have fun.

When creating your budget be sure to create both a monthly budget and an annual budget. According to Budgeting.Thenest.com, "A dynamic budget, or one that changes projections each month as you input your income and expense, will help you keep track of your finances and avoid falling short of important life goals such as saving for retirement, buying a home or starting a college fund for your children." [25]

---

25   Sam Ashe-Edmunds, "Importance of Keeping a Budget," *budgeting.the-nest.com.* 2020.

An annual budget, which is also known as a dynamic budget, creates your family's financial picture, controls your long-term spending, helps you save, and projects the reality of your situation. You can plan and spend in January because you know in August back-to-school shopping for your children will cause strain on the family budget.

It may even reflect where most of your money is lost. Once October rolls in and the holidays come you will see more financial strain. You are still in the hole from August! Knowing the potential problem in January can help your family to make more adjustments that work in your favor. You will be empowered to make decisions that will keep your family on budget and out of the doghouse.

Remember these tips to help you be a better planner. Financial success is dependent on your ability to plan a goal and execute it. Look at the list below and figure what area you need to build more muscles in and go back and reread that area. Changing your mindset in these areas will help you to be better planners and better doers.

- Embrace Your Imperfection
- Beat Wishful Thinking
- Beat Deadline Stress
- Cut the Goal in Half
- Be Realistic
- Overcome the Balancing Act
- You Can't Do It All

CHAPTER 4

PEOPLE

———

When you decide to level up and change your life for the better, you will lose friends along the way.

Losing my best friend was uncomfortable, but it was necessary for personal growth. Cutting that cord was difficult. I wish I could tell you everyone will be rooting for you to succeed on your financial journey. Negative people are a part of life, but it feels different when they are close to you. Not everyone will get it. Paying off debt is reserved for special occasions such as buying a new house. Chasing wealth is still considered taboo. Living below your means makes you strange.

Purpose, passion, planning, and people are severely crucial areas for your success with money. The psychological effects of people will make you or break you. Your journey is not exclusive to only you.

I read a book called The Energy Bus: Ten Rules to Fuel Your Life, Work, and Team with Positive Energy and it was a fictious story about a gentleman named George. George was in a rut until he met this bus driver named Joy. She taught him ten rules to change his circumstances. One rule stood out to me as it relates to finances. Rule four was "Invite People on your Bus and Share Your Vision for the Road Ahead." [26]

The truth is your financial freedom is dependent on the people around you. Your tribe will either build you up or tear you down. This part of the book applies to every personal relationship in your life. Reflect on each part of your journey and figure out who should be on this ride and for how long.

People either replenish your energy or deplete you, but the good news is you can control it. If you do not allow it, it does not happen. The three groups that people fall into are: family, friends, and foes.

FAMILY

Family are people you cannot choose. The people you share your home with and have the same blood running through your veins are the people closest to you, but they can hurt you the most because of that close bond. Having support in this area during your journey will provide a significant mental boost and will give you a strong sense of purpose and encouragement to not give up with when times are hard. On the shadow side of that, they can drain your energy the most and make it extremely difficult to progress toward your financial goals. If they choose to abandon you, talk about you, or even worse, pretend to support you, it could emotionally handicap you.

---

26 Jon Gordon, *The Energy Bus: 10 Rules to Fuel Your Life, Work, and Team with Positive Energy* (Chichester, West Sussex: Wiley, 2015).

I was blessed to have my mom in my corner. Though she never accomplished what I was pursuing, she was always there for me. Search your family and see if you have anyone that can support you on your journey toward financial freedom. The people in your family will always be a source of inspiration because whether you like it or not, they are connected to your "why."

"Call it a clan, call it a network, call it a tribe, call it a family. Whatever you call it, whoever you are, you need one."

JANE HOWARD

The people in this group will be your best cheerleaders or your worst haters. You must mentally prepare for both options. Depression and anger are two emotional states that will come along when your family hurts you. I sat down and interviewed many people in debt, and six out of ten said they were alone on this journey when asked if they have support from their family to become financially free. The odds are against you in this department, but that does not mean it is over for you. I was blessed to have my mother's support along the way. If you have no one in your family corner, God created friends just for you that will fill in for family.

FRIENDS

Friends are subject to your approval.

Whoever you decide to call a friend reflects upon you. Although friends can be family, most friends will not share the same bloodline. A great friend in a moment of need is priceless. Show me your group of friends, and I can show you your future.

Jim Rohn stated, "You are the average of the five people you spend the most time with." [27] This a powerful statement. See, we have a messianic complex where we believe we can be a savior to our friends, but studies show that the Bible was right in 1 Corinthians 15:33: "bad behavior corrupts good company." According to an article written on Insider.com, "Bad friendships can increase your risk for diseases such as depression, heart disease, diabetes, and cancer. Also, unhealthy lifestyle habits can spread in close friend groups." [28]

One Sunday morning in Palo Alto, California, there was a mass arrest amongst college students for Penal Code 211, armed robbery, and Penal Code 459, burglary. It was the beginning of what we call today as the Stanford Experiment. There was a separate group of college students who were blindfolded and hauled down to the station to be prisoners and prison guards.

The students were chosen based on a local ad that they responded to about the psychological effects of becoming a prisoner or a correctional officer. Stanford went all the way to create this fake prison environment to simulate prison. Seventy people answered this ad, but they ended up with twenty-four to go through the experiment. The group was split in half—twelve prisoners and twelve correctional officers. Both

---

27 Aimee Groth, "You're the Average of the Five People You Spend the Most Time With," *Business Insider* (2012).
28 Yvette Manes, "5 Ways Toxic Friendships Could Be Hurting Your Health," *Insider*, 2020.

groups were monitored, but they were not aware of it. Philip Zimbardo created this experiment to last two weeks, but it ended in six days. Below is an excerpt from the official website of the psychology experiment.

"At this point, it became clear that we had to end the study. We had created an overwhelmingly powerful situation—a situation in which prisoners were withdrawing and behaving in unhealthy ways, and in which some of the guards were behaving sadistically. Even the 'good' guards felt helpless to intervene, and none of the guards quit while the study was in progress. First, we had learned through videotapes that the guards were escalating their abuse of prisoners in the middle of the night when they thought no researchers were watching, and the experiment was 'off'." [29]

An experiment like this has never been repeated, but it is an example of how negative people and bad intentions can affect good in anyone. If your friends have poor spending habits and you hang with them all the time, you will follow their lead. Remember, you are the average of them. If everyone around you is broke and stuck with a poor financial mindset, you are not too far behind. On the flip side, if you surround yourself with positive, like-minded people, the synergy between you and friends will help you all reach your goals. People often overlook the people in their life during their financial freedom journey. Friends are one of the essential relationships in the people group. The mindset you need to have in this department is a business mindset.

---

29   Zimbardo, Philip. 1971.The Stanford Prison Experiment.Research, Stanford: Stanford University.

Pretend you are starting a business. We all know that great companies excel based on the people inside of them. I have been a part of some large organizations, such as Speedway and Macy's, in management. I learned as a leader you will not get far without a great team. Becoming debt-free is similar, choose your friends wisely. You have a choice in this area. You cannot choose your family, but you can, for sure, pick your friends.

FOES

Every great story has an antagonist. Do not be alarmed when people come against you. Everyone will not be on the same page you are on. If being financially free was the norm, debt would not be such a problem in the US We live in a world where instant gratification is our norm. People no longer consider thinking about their legacy. This finite mindset hinders people from seeing the big picture. If you are not careful, it will cripple you too. You will become hostage to what others say about you. You need to be strong mentally and trust that your "why" is strong enough. Remember that people are rooting for you.

The reality for some is there aren't family or friends in their corner; and they are doing this alone. If that is the case for you, you must turn the negative energy from your foes as motivation to keep going. Trust that your purpose is more significant than their fear, doubt, and lies. Those who cannot support your dream can add a lot of stress if you are diligent in playing offense against them. They can be family members, ex-friends, colleagues, and strangers. These are people who you know dislike you for whatever reason, are biased against you, and have shown signs of ill will. You must cut them off and remove them from your life immediately.

FEELINGS CHECK

Below is a list of the type of feeling stress induces when your foes are getting to you:

- irritable, impatient, overburdened, aggressive
- neglected, lonely
- unable to compromise
- depressed
- unable to enjoy yourself
- nervous, anxious, or afraid

Take an inventory of how you feel as often as you need to. Mental health is real, and so is stress. Stress is created from resisting situations intended to foster change. Our inability to grow creates stress. For example, when my wife and I lost our child, and we got hit with a huge hospital bill. But more importantly, we had to pick up the emotional pieces to rebuild our family. That situation put us under a lot of pressure, both financially and emotionally. Losing a loved one is never easy, especially an unborn child. For those who have lost a child, my heart goes out to you. When you take that pain and mix it with debt, all you can do is hang your head low. I get it. However, you cannot stay in that place. You must move forward and trust that things will get better.

THE FOUR CS YOU NEED IN YOUR LIFE

I had the honor and privilege to sit down and listen to Jeremiah Castille live; Jeremiah is the chaplain of the University of Alabama's powerhouse football team. Jeremiah played as a corner-back before being drafted in the NFL by the Tampa Bay Buccaneers. He was a third round pick of the NFL Draft in 1983. Jeremiah was number eight out of nine children. His parents only had a fourth-grade education, and his home was filled with domestic violence and drug abuse, but he made it.

During the Truth at Work Conference in 2019, Jeremiah shared some wisdom he learned from Bear Bryant, and what he learned in his six years in the NFL. To my surprise, he did not discuss football. He described people and how to put the right people in your life to become successful. The people in your life will not only make you successful, but they will also keep you motivated during your journey.

"How do you go from tough circumstances in your life to accomplishment?" asked Jeremiah.

Becoming financially independent is a significant accomplishment. The people you are attached to either add value to your life or take value away. To help you choose what kind of people to put into your journey there are four categories. The pursuit of excellence is a high cost, and relationships matter.

CULTURE
That intangible stickiness, something you cannot measure, what attracts others to you, are descriptions I call culture. Believe it or not, you can control how others see you. You begin by changing how you perceive yourself. Think about what message you want to send to others financially. Do you want to be known as a party animal or a free meal ticket, or when people see you, all they see is a good time at no cost? You attract what you want to see. There should be some common themes that should be in your culture.

You need a culture of excellence. Excellence precedes influence. Culture opens the door for you to share your beliefs, attitudes, values, and best practices. So, if the vision is motivational, it will be shared by everyone on the journey, and people can hold you accountable to it. Excellence is sticking to that budget you set for yourself. Excellence is preparing your mind to live beyond what you see today, but always repositioning for the future. Excellence is controlling your spending and balancing your needs vs. your wants. If excellence is demanded in your circle and during your journey, people will either respect that or remove themselves from the atmosphere you created.

Every day we have an opportunity and obligation to be excellent in all our doings. Tell your friend or your family member that you love them, but that you demand excellence. You may not be perfect 100 percent of the time, but the goal will always be pursing excellence 100 percent of the time. Having an infinite mindset is another critical part you can add to the culture while on your journey. The finite mind is untrustworthy because it only sees wins and losses at that moment.

There will be times during your journey where you drop the ball but having an infinite mindset will allow you to see that as an opportunity, not a defeat. People in your circle that push this into the culture will help you stay in the marathon, not in the race.

Simon Sinek stated in The Infinite Game that to ask, "What's best for me?" is finite thinking, and "What's best for us? is infinite thinking." [30]

---

30   Simon Sinek.*Start with The Why*.Portfolio; Reprint edition (December 27, 2011).

When you have an eye out for more than just yourself, it adds a lot of value to any relationship. Could you imagine dating someone, better yet marrying someone, and all they cared about was themselves? Financially there is no difference. You need people in your circle that know and respect what you are trying to do. For example, I had to cut off a close friend of mind because all he wanted was to go out to parties and drink. How does that fit into my culture? Living that way is expensive when shots cost ten dollars a pop with a discount, and it does not honor my wife. If I tell her, "We are committed to getting out of debt," and she sees me spending fifty to a hundred dollars at bars, she will not believe in my vision, and thus she will not follow me. Worse yet, that might cause her to revolt and spend money on things she deems okay that are outside the vision as well.

Removing people who plan to inject toxic pollutants into your culture is okay. You must protect your culture at all costs. It might take a long time to build up, but it can be gone with a snap of a finger. Pursuing excellence with an infinite mindset is a healthy combo. Combining these two things will help your culture dictate who deserves to be on your financial journey to freedom and who does not.

Ray serves as this person for me in my life. I was not blessed to grow up with two parents, but when you have the right mindset, that does not matter. I mentally adopted his parents like my own, and I have watched their relationship and the culture they have set for their children to prosper. Ray opens the door for extreme support and truth for me. He got those values from his parents, and now I get to experience them. There is nothing in the world that I can ask for that he would not share, and the feeling is mutual. That comradery is so vital because financial journeys are full of ups and downs.

CHARACTER

Whenever there are two paths and one is right, the other is wrong. No matter what the reward is at the end of the road, pick right. When you are living paycheck to paycheck, it is understandable to want to get fast money; however, you must ask yourself: at what cost? Character is your life on display. When people see what you are doing it is sometimes irrelevant because it is easy to pretend. However, when it is just you and your thoughts the real you comes out. Hold yourself to high standards because you submit to God, not man, and he sees all things. High character is a must and it is the foundation of your being.

We are all one wrong decision away from ruining everything. The last thing we need is for someone in our circle to tempt us to make that wrong choice. Be proactive and look for character among those in your presence. Do not get caught up in someone's reputation. Abraham Lincoln said, "Character is like a tree and the reputation like a shadow. The shadow is what we think of it; the tree is the real thing."31 Look for trees, not shadows.

Your financial journey will build character inside of you because of the things you have to endure. It is not easy to put the work in to destroy debt. It is not easy to withstand the

31 Daniel Mark Epstein,*The Lincolns: Portrait of a Marriage* (New York: Ballantine Books, 2009).

emotional punches you might get when life hits you upside the head. It is not easy to keep your mind focused on your purpose, while the stress of life is blocking your thoughts like the Great Smog of 1952. Trust that the work is worth it. Take care of your mental health by embracing the people in the circle who are rooting for your success. Know in the end that because of character, the people around you will hold themselves to a higher standard just like you!

Do not waste your time recruiting low character people into your circle. Do the right thing, even if it costs you. We all know what that right thing is and what that wrong thing is in the heart of hearts. God has given us an internal GPS to navigate those decisions.

I was tempted to sell drugs to reach my debt-free status early, but at what cost? Going to jail, getting robbed, or even worse: killed. I am glad I had friends and family to reinforce that I did not need to resort to that. My character is the foundation of who I am, not the debt, not a bill, or anything else. I had to stay the course and do what was right. Your character is what gives you your credibility. "Jeremiah is debt-free, but he stepped on others to get there." How would that story sound? Do not let that be your story.

Bernard and Jonathan serve as these friends for me in this area. During some of the darkest moments of my journey, I was tempted to sway off course. I knew the expectations from them were to exemplify high character, especially when no one was looking. These men are not perfect, but they are transparent with me, and we guide each other's lives together. Their lives were examples for me to live by, and they were my accountability partners. Their relationship with God positively impacted me and helped me keep my mind on what really matters most. Embracing opportunities to be a better husband, better steward, and how to be the same man in front of thousands as I am in front of one are some of the things that kept me grounded during my journey.

CONFIDENCE

You do not fall into success, you prepare for it. Confidence is gradual through effort and decision-making. The people around you need to have faith. They must believe that you will hit your goal, and they will hit theirs too. When you are in the valleys of life, a quick reminder to believe in yourself will pull you out of the rut. Depression and stress hinder the expression of confidence. Remember when you were an adolescent, and you had to take the SAT. The people who studied for it and believed they were ready had confidence. The kids who had no support, no training, or no help felt hopeless. That hopelessness breeds depression which leads to self-doubt.

Confident people on your journey are your muscle group to keep moving forward. Let us study an animal with supreme confidence. A lion is not called the king of the jungle for nothing. A lion has confidence. When he sees an elephant, he sees dinner. His mind does not second guess his ability to take down an elephant. An elephant is a massive beast in comparison to the lion. One stomp from its foot could crush a lion, but one thing separates the lion from the elephant. It is the confidence of the lion. The lion is not concerned about the physical attributes of the elephant. All the lion sees is dinner.

We can learn something from that mentality. It does not matter how massive the debt may be or where you are on the journey. You must possess the confidence to proceed with the plan of attack. Your situation is controlled by how you perceive it. Change your mindset and improve your mental health by just believing you can do it. That debt is dinner!

I had an opportunity to sit with a family that was $35,000 in debt. Their circumstance paralyzed the family. The wife had less income due to her health, and the finances just slipped away. She felt terrible because her husband trusted her with the money, and she "thought" she lost control. Those things might be a fact but remember your infinite mindset. The game is not over. I proceeded to let her know planning and changing her mindset was all she needed to regain her confidence to knock out the debt. She only lacked the confidence to get her family back on track. Lyme disease robbed her of her physical strength and allowed her health to be compromised by stress, anxiety, and pain. It was amazing to see how just being a support system and giving them confidence changed the trajectory of their finances and, better yet, their overall lives. By the grace of God and staying the course she knocked out the debt and the Lyme! I live for moments like those because it fuels me to keep fighting and pushing on my journey to help people win with money.

Having the right people in your corner who are confident can help you see beyond your problems and help you get back on track. Look for the lions in your circle and thank them! Iron truly does sharpen iron, so pick confident people to walk with you during your journey to financial freedom. The people you pick will create your support system that root for your during your financial journey.

"Cultivating and maintaining a social support system will benefit you throughout each of your life's endeavors. Support networks do more than offer a sense of community and belonging—they can also help you achieve academic and professional success." [32] Thank God for support systems!

My wife, Selam, serves as my friend in this area. She believes in me so much! I know everyone might not be married, but if you have people pouring into you and believing in you during the journey, that is all you need. Throughout our journey, my wife stayed firm and trusted me to lead us out because she knew who was leading me. There were moments when I wanted to give up, but she encouraged me and helped me see the better days ahead.

A weak mindset may trigger the fear of failing, but a healthy mindset looks at it as an opportunity to succeed.

Do you have a Selam? They do not need to be a spouse. They can be whoever you want them to be.

COURAGE

Jeremiah Castille defined courage as "the ability to conquer the unknown." This definition stood out to me because it takes courage to tackle debt. Especially when it is six figures.

---

32 Herzing Staff, "Why Your Support System Is Important for Your Success." Herzing University, June 8, 2017.

It is easy to ignore the issue and live life like everyone else. Courage takes grit and will not allow you to give up. God told Joshua to be strong and courageous. He told him this three times. But that last verse always jumped off the page to me. I want to share it with you below.

Joshua 1:9 "Have I not commanded? Be strong and of good courage; do not be afraid, nor be dismayed, for the Lord your God is with you wherever you go."

That verse has so much power! When someone tells you that they are with you, it comforts you. It helps you fight. You need courageous people on your journey to fight with you and encourage you to keep going when things get tough. Life will happen, but you must go on. This comfort and peace are like no other and will kick depression, stress, anxiety, and any other negative emotions out your mind.

When I shattered my elbow, I felt like giving up, but the courage of my wife would not let me. The support of my physical therapist would not let me. The courage of my daughter kept me moving forward. Courage is contagious and magnetic. The more you have, the better. You also need someone to tell you when you are messing up. That takes courage, too, because it is an uncomfortable conversation.

My brother Keon serves as a friend in this area. Though we do not talk as much as we should, I cannot think of anyone as fearless as my brother. As a cop in Gary, Indiana you must be prepared for anything! Even though that is a sign of courage, I saw his heart on display as he raised three kids on his own as a single dad. Though he received great support from my auntie, it takes guts to raise two daughters and a son on your own. That courage speaks volumes silently, and when we do talk, I always pull a nugget out of him to use as leverage to go harder on my personal journey.

If you do not have any of the types of friends mentioned above, as you get started on your path, those friends will be revealed to you. Be open and receptive to the new people you are attracting after making room and throwing out the old unnecessary ones.

CHOOSE THEM WISELY

There is no limit to how many people can be on your journey. The key is to appreciate how small or large your circle is. You need family, friends, and even foes to help push you toward your financial goals. Remember the impact of the four Cs when you are choosing your tribe. There will be times when your tribe needs to be reevaluated. Seasons change, and so do people. Do not be afraid to put yourself first and uphold what you value most. This is not anyone else's journey to financial freedom, it's yours.

CHAPTER 5

PERSISTENCE

___

"You will always be broke! Debt is a part of life. You will owe someone until you die."

If someone tells you this, these are lies, lies, and, I repeat, all lies.

Do you remember why you are doing what you set out to do?

Your purpose will feel like you are being tested if it is authentic. The universe will use different events to raise you into alignment with the blessings that you are attracting. The old you, your old thoughts patterns and beliefs must be surrendered for you to step into the new life you desire. Therefore, staying focused and positive is essential. Every thought you have welcomes a new experience. Your attitude toward life creates expectations. Life will always fulfill the expectations you have.

When you said you wanted your life to be different, the universe heard that. When you made your plans, the universe recorded that. The universe will be serious about serving you according to God's will when you show your faith through action.

My journey was not perfect. I had plenty of setbacks. Throughout this book, I have shared the relevant parts the defined my journey. I want to make sure that you understand that it took a lot. Not only to write this book, but to have this testimony to share with you.

THE TRUE TEST BEGINS NOW

Persistence is the grit to fight through when others settle and accept defeat. The refusal to give up will knock down any barrier. No one can stop you from achieving your goal. You will stand against any opposition and be victorious.

Imagine a boxer in the final round with no energy left, but he refuses to throw in the towel. You keep pushing no matter what you hear or what people say. Muhammad Ali was known for outlasting his competition by tiring them out and enduring the best punches they had to throw, then he amazed the crowd and delivered a fatal blow to his opponent to win the fight in the end! Do not give up under any circumstances; keep fighting.

I remember sitting down in my one-bedroom apartment, thinking about what I was going to do. I had a wife and a daughter. We wanted a larger family one day. And I was stuck here in this one-bedroom apartment with all of us sleeping in the same bed. Yes, we had two fancy cars. Those fancy cars came with two big car notes. My priorities were off, but I was beginning to accept that.

WHEN YOUR JOURNEY IS TESTED

At that moment, I began to say enough is enough. I was turning the ship around, but life happened.

Boom!

My wife had a car crash.

One fancy car gone. In the blink of an eye it was totaled. We didn't have any gap coverage. Gap insurance is needed when your vehicle is worth less than what you owe on it. We had to roll that equity into a new car. Our debt climbed.

I was not trying to get a new car. I was trying to get an old car. I was trying to follow the Dave Ramsey plan. However, you get what you pay for, and I couldn't refinance the difference. I was upside down on the car my wife wrecked. The balance left on the car was more than the car was worth. I had two choices: get a personal loan to pay off the car or roll the negative equity into a new car. I chose option two because I didn't qualify for the personal loan.

The car was modest: a three-year-old Nissan Altima. My car payment was now $356 a month.

Boom!

Another car crash and the same result followed all within six months. This time, I had to learn the virtue of resilience. Our total car debt went from $30,000 to $58,000, but I didn't give up. I refused to let my story end that way.

You may have experienced something like this, or you may be going through it right now. You may have had a few of your own "boom" moments. Look in the mirror and ask yourself: "What is the universe trying to teach me? What is the God trying to reveal to me?" Let the universe know you mean business, and God's will for you will prevail. Spend time in the mirror and give yourself pep talks by using these affirmations.

I am going to get this done by any means necessary.

I will be financially free, and my family will experience success.

I will be the lender instead of the borrower.

Psychologist Carol Dweck coined a theory on mindsets. She stated that people fall in a fixed mindset (poor) or a growth mindset (rich). People with a fixed mindset avoid challenges and give up during obstacles because their level of thinking is static. People with a growth mindset embrace challenges and persist during setbacks.

Your financial journey is determined by your mindset. I can't say that enough.

A poor mindset sees delays, becomes discouraged, and gives up. A rich mindset learns from setbacks and perseveres. Throughout your day, you make a choice between poor or rich. A poor mindset leads to poor mental health. When you give into depression, stress, and hopelessness, you eat away at your success.

I want to share a story—that most might not realize happened—before we go deep into those mindsets.

In July of 1965 near Bristol in Southwest England, a little girl named J.K. Rowling was born. Her father worked at Rolls Royce as an aircraft engineer. Her mother was a science technician in the chemistry department at Wyedean Comprehensive. J.K. Rowling lost her mother to multiple sclerosis in 1990. She was only twenty-five, on the brink of womanhood, and she lost her biggest role model.

During that hard time, the little girl's love of books helped her through the mourning process. A natural bookworm, she wrote her first book at the age of six. It was a simple story about a rabbit. The title of the story was Rabbit. At the age of eleven, she wrote her first novel about seven crushed diamonds and the people who owned them. She was a child prodigy that would have a few trials in life, such as her mother's death, a divorce, and life as a single mom. As a single mother, she was forced to be on welfare to take care of her daughter. None of that stopped her. The same year her mother died she began writing one a piece of literature that went on to build a best-selling franchise. J.K. Rowling began to write Harry Potter.

It took seven years to get it published, but it caught fire quickly and continued to grow. She's sold 500 million copies and counting since its release!

Her struggles were behind her, and she could finally say she made it and reached her goal. Rowling began her writing journey in 1971 and it took off in 1997. J.K. Rowling's rich mindset helped her pursue her dream without giving up. Dealing with rejection and negativity is hard, but it can be handled. A rich mindset will help you push through on your financial journey and help experience true financial freedom.

FIXED MINDSET VS. GROWTH MINDSET

A fixed mindset boxes you in, and it makes everything around you appear finite. A key thing to capture with a fixed mindset is how you view obstacles. Obstacles represent a brick wall, and you will give up if you have this mindset. Challenges bring the fear of failure, and that pressure is too much to take on with a fixed mindset.

Instead, let us pursue a growth mindset. We must embrace those challenges as opportunities to grow and learn. The growth mindset is packed with lessons and inspirations to share with others. At first, it will be hard to change your old thought patterns. As you read books, find motivational speakers, and develop healthy habits it will become easier to build your growth mindset—this is how I began to look at my financial journey. I knew the times were shaky, but I imagined all the people I could help with my testimony and financial success.

Mental Wealth is a new mindset
that we need to have concerning our
financial situation.

Do not allow your five senses to give all the confirmation that you are on the right path. Look within yourself and receive confirmation from God to keep moving forward. Renewing your mind to the truth of who you are will shape your financial mindset. You will have peace instead of stress, joy instead of sadness, and hope instead of depression.

"The Lord himself goes before you and will be with you; he will never leave you nor forsake you. Do not be afraid; do not be discouraged." Deuteronomy 31:8.

Your story will end on a good note when you shift your mindset. I know this because I know the author. The author of our story is God.

When God puts his name on a creation, you know that it will be seen through to completion. God breathe greatness inside you on the day you were born. I wrote this book to motivate you to keep going and know that a change in mindset will pay off that debt. Changing your mindset will change your lifestyle. You might have to live on less than you make or get some additional income sources. Driving for Uber or Lyft, freelancing, selling candles, making jewelry, and good old babysitting are all options for you to make more money. Whatever your side hustle is, remember it is just a means to an end. If you do not have a side hustle, find one. The goal is to get active and move closer to your goal.

IT IS NOT HOW YOU START; IT IS HOW YOU FINISH.
June of 2009 will forever be a summer I will never forget. It is a familiar story for people in the 219 area code. A tale of

what could have happened. A story of great potential thrown away because of drugs, sex, or murder. The kind of story that makes you cry and wonder why. I was blessed to play in this simple story but have a different ending. My story started typically but ended uniquely special. The story is a testimony to the strength that I would need to pull from to complete this financial journey.

I am from East Chicago, Indiana, a neighboring city to Gary, Indiana. Some people may know Gary but never heard of East Chicago. Gary became the murder capital in 1993, with ninety-one killings per 100,000 residents. East Chicago was not far behind. East Chicago was a cold, harsh place to grow up, but that city built a lot of resilience in me.

I never knew my father. My grandfather was my father, but when I was sixteen cancer took my grandfather away. I was forced to deal with his death in silence. I feared no one would understand what he truly meant to me. As a young man, the responsibilities at hand were too great to handle. My mom's worst fear came true. Her only son, a young black male still in high school, was having a baby!

Like any mother, she was devastated and felt like my life was over. At that time, it felt like she hated me. In hindsight, I realize it was more disappointment mixed with accepting that I was not her little boy anymore. My mom wrote me off. I would be lying to you if I told you that it did not hurt. Our deteriorating relationship took a toll on my self-worth, and there were verbal attacks. Maybe she was right. My mental health was on the brink of collapsing but I could not let that stop me.

Even without a support system, I needed just to keep going. I graduated as the valedictorian of my class in 2009 with a child on the way. I took all the negativity from my mother and depression to fuel me. I focused on becoming the best father I could be!

I never had a chance to enjoy my accomplishments. People told me that I was number one at the bottom. East Chicago Central was full of young men that society had already given up on; being a valedictorian there did not mean anything —that school was easy. The teachers hated their jobs and us. I had negativity coming at me from all angles. I used what others proclaimed about my education to plant seeds in my garden.

TURNING POINT

When you make a poor financial decision, it is impacting your future and your now. The root of those decisions relates to mental health. How you feel affects your actions. Therefore, to turn the ship around, you must change that mindset.

I was once listening to a podcast featuring the rapper Kevin Gates. He shared financial advice. He learned the hard way because he blew a lot of money early on in his rap career. He stated his greatest lesson was the ten times rule. The ten times rule simply means if you cannot purchase ten of them, you cannot afford it.[33]

---

33   "Kevin Gates on the Worst Money He's Ever Blown | Men's Wealth | Men's Health," YouTube Video,YouTube, November 21, 2019.

That advice changed his life. Maybe that advice can change your life. A lot of people go for retail therapy to fix an issue that needs actual therapists. Instant gratification will not solve what is hurting you or causing you to be depressed. Sadly, a new house does not make a new home. A new car still has the same old driver. A new purse still carries the same identification. Money cannot buy you happiness. One of my favorite quotes is from Jim Carrey. He said, "I think everyone should get rich and famous and do everything they ever dreamed of so they can see that it's not the answer." That quote has so much power. Jim Carrey has never lost touch with what is truly important.

You are on this journey for a reason. Your purpose does matter. Be persistent and see it through. I am not telling you to live on rice and beans for three years. Getting a steak dinner is okay. But you must remain persistent. Taking a trip to celebrate a significant milestone is okay, but do not let that stop you from achieving your goals. Follow the plan you set for yourself and your family—it is so easy to get thrown off track.

The American dream is the gasoline to the machine of capitalism. The dream is all built on marketing to you and telling you what you need to be happy. Buying items to make you feel good is poor mental health. I remember buying $100 dress shirts to make up for my self-confidence. I went broke building this false image of myself, and I realized later in life that $100 dress shirts get the same dirty collar as the $20 dress shirt. A healthy mindset is your greatest asset and worth more than diamonds and gold.

We live in a world full of abundance. When you wake up and the alarm clock goes off, you realize every day you have a decision to make. But remember every decision you make today is not just about today. It also impacts your future. Do not become a generational thief robbing from your future generations. I refuse to let that be my story. And I refuse to let that be your story.

Go back to each chapter, whichever chapter you feel you need clarity from and reread it. If you are unsure of how you find your "why," reread the sections on purpose. If you need to hit your goals and your plan is failing, read the parts about planning until you get it. If you do not know how to distinguish what kind of people you need in your life, reread the section on people. If you are falling short on talking to our Creator and being grateful, take this very moment to be thankful. Lastly, if you need a motivational pep talk, reread this chapter on persistence.

There is nothing in this world that can stop you from reaching your financial goals, other than you. Enough is enough. You should be tired of living like this. Your vision of freedom should be motivation for you to keep going until you cross the finish line. It took you a long time to get into this mess, and it might take you a long time to get out of this mess. But it is okay; we are ready for that.

I know what you have been reading may sound like a rant, but it is near and dear to my heart. It disappoints me to see people mentally broken and emotionally defeated by their finances. You have the heart to help others, but you can't afford to.

Becoming financially free is like working out. You are not going to get that summer body in one day, no matter how good your genes are. You must put the work in. You must go to the gym. You must do the sit-ups, you must do the bench press, you must do the curls, and you must do the squats. Your body will respond to consistency and dedication. That is the core of persistence; we must push through the soreness of our journey and keep going to that financial gym.

I will be praying for you during this journey. I do not know if other people are praying for you. But please remember I am praying for you every day, because I know what it takes to get rid of a substantial financial problem. $210,711 is a lot of stupid. Persistence helped me cross that line to financial freedom.

YOUR DAY WILL COME

On September 16th, 2019, my family's life changed forever. Our past was gone, and the future was shining. It was the day I made the last payment to the law office for my wife's car accident lawsuit. The final payment was $5,000. I had been saving up some money and praying for a miracle. I did not want to pay this because I knew the accident was not her fault, but our cheap insurance company did not adequately cover the incident.

I reached out to the debt agency and made an offer lower than the amount owed to be free and clear of the debt. The phone call went smoothly; the lady that answered my call said she would call me back after she spoke to her boss about accepting the offer. I was a nervous wreck those few hours while I was waiting. Was I indeed moments away from being debt-free?

I received a call, and her answer solidified my vision I created five years ago. She said, "Yes!" I kept my composure, and she told me I had seven days to send in the money. I sent it in three. God did indeed answer my prayer. I was in awe; our time had come. The first thing I thought about was telling my wife. She carried some guilt from the accident because it put us further in debt. No matter how much I loved her, she still carried that burden. On September 16th, the responsibility was gone.

I called my wife immediately after the call. She could not even believe it. Part of me wished I had waited so I could see her face, but I could not hold it in. We paid $5,000 on the $20,951.07 we owed, and we were done. I asked my wife to toast to the next chapter of our lives. We do not owe anyone else anything. The last $5,000 electronic transfer felt good. In those moments, we felt peace, gratitude, and achievement. If we could do this, we could do anything. It was incredible, humbling. I remember driving home in awe. My wife and I paid off over $200,000 of debt.

That dream of financial freedom became a reality. Something else happened to me that day. It was like something came over me. Like I drank the "Secret Stuff" from *Space Jam*.[34] I felt a joy that I cannot even put into words. I found my sweet spot. I knew I had to dedicate my life to this. I knew that God created me and took me through this crazy path, so I can

---

34 *Space Jam* (Warner Bros. Pictures, 1996).

help other people focus on the 80 percent rather than the 20 percent when it comes to money.

All the sacrifices and all the tears were all worth it. Whenever I tried to cheat the process, get money quickly by playing poker, or do other dumb things, it never worked. I was foolish to think cheating could work. You must be persistent in following your plan and taking all life has for you. Take care of your mind by focusing on what truly matters.

Most big wins do not come from lottery tickets, casino nights, sports betting, and any other quick fix to avoid hard work. None of those detours were a part of my journey. It might not be a part of yours either, or you must be okay with it. Keep up the hard work!

For you to be persistent on your journey, you need the right people in your life as we get ready to talk about people in the next chapter. Take inventory of who is in your life and why they are in your life. Who are your friends, family, colleagues? Every person you interact with becomes a part of life.

CHAPTER 6

PRAYER

———

According to a Barna Group report, 62 percent of people pray during Thanksgiving for gratitude. This is number one reason why people pray in America. Surprisingly, finances were not on their list of reasons to pray at all. I believe these two areas should be blended to produce the perfect mindset for your financial freedom.

There may come a time during your journey that you become completely exhausted. You may feel like there is nothing more you can give. In these moments you may feel the loneliest you have ever felt. We face these challenges because we miss all the stops signs that were warning us to slow down and rest. We are too attached to our worldly accomplishments, our relationships, our to-do lists, and our illusions of the world. We need rest. We must return to our creator and doing that comes from looking within.

Implementing prayer is not optional, it is required.

Prayer is something that too many people overlook.

If you had all the tools necessary to create a better situation for yourself, you would have done it. You must let go of feelings of unworthiness and surrender to faith and believe that your plans will be accomplished. The motivation you need to succeed does not come from hard work alone; it always comes from your faith in God. I know I could not have made it through this journey to financial freedom without prayer. Prayer was the energy source that kept me going.

WHY SHOULD YOU PRAY

Can you recognize miracles, blessings, or answered prayers?

There is no such thing as luck, good or bad. Your faith, beliefs, emotions, and thoughts all form the life that you experience. God gave us free will to consciously choose positive thoughts, pleasant feelings, and to trust in God's power to overcome all external circumstances. Every person in your life is intended to foster growth within you, even if you are unable to see how.

When you pray, it heals mind and spirit. Prayer heals the negative emotions, thoughts, and beliefs that keep you from obtaining your goals. Once healed you are forever changed and able to pursue other goals that foster growth and the fulfillment of your life objectives. Your desire for a better life is the will of God, which pushes you forward to expand and create a life of abundance, peace, and charity. Answered prayers come in all forms, precisely in a way that will be for you to understand. God will always communicate with you in a way that you understand.

"The power of affirmative prayer sets in motion a process of healing false beliefs that prevents an individual from fully realizing their spiritual inheritance. Prayer is an intimate communion with the Spirit in the language of one's own heart." (Agape International Spiritual Center n.d.)[35]

The language of your heart is personal just like your financial journey. God is the only one who truly understands how you feel and what you need to hear or see to push you past your fear or doubt.

WHAT TO PRAY ABOUT

Prayer is personal and straightforward. It does not have to be overly complicated. It can be anything from pure silence to 1,000-plus words. It's your conversation with God. I said prayers as short as "God, help me to thank God for everything I have." A prayer of gratitude can reposition your mind to focus on the things you do have not the things you do not have. This type of prayer removes stress and anxiety and takes you to a place of peace and adoration. Here are some things to be thankful during your journey:

- Healing and perfect health
- A peaceful mind
- The abundance you currently have
- Prosperity for your family member and friends
- Gratitude for your life thus far

---

35 "Agape Spiritual Principles and Practices," AgapeLive, 2020.

- Guidance in accomplishing goals
- Your job as an opportunity to earn money
- Waking up every morning
- Having all your senses
- Fresh flowers
- Simply being alive

There is a lot of power in writing out what you're grateful for and physically seeing it, then verbalizing it. Oprah Winfrey lives by this idea. She started her own gratitude journal back in 1996, and I am sure she keeps one to this day. In one episode of The Oprah Winfrey Show she said, "For years I've advocated keeping a gratitude journey, writing down five things every day that brought pleasure and gratefulness."

Oprah has also said, "the more thankful I became, the more my bounty increased. That is because, for sure, what you focus on expands. When you focus on the goodness in life, you create more of it." [36]

Prayers of thankfulness and gratitude create a peaceful mind and a loving heart. Having these two virtues throughout your financial journey is priceless. When life hits you, your reflex response should always be to give thanks and gratitude. For instance, when I shattered my elbow playing basketball, I was grateful because at least I did not fall on my head! In that split second of dropping out the air, I had enough reflexes to try and break my fall. However, shattering my head or cracking my skull might have had fatal complications. Who

36 Oprah Winfrey, "Oprah's Gratitude Journal Oprah's Lifeclass Oprah Winfrey Network," YouTube Video,YouTube, October 26, 2013.

knows what could have happened? We will never know, and I am thankful for that.

Another example is with the four-car accident my wife was in. That could've resulted in her death. Thank God we don't have to tell that story. Choose to see the good and thank God for the results, because it always could've been worse. Whatever your pains might be right now, remain positive. It might take a while to heal from those wounds but embrace the journey—that is real Mental Wealth!

I recommend keeping a gratitude journal and writing at least five things you're grateful for every day. Read it daily before your prayer time and use it to help you stay focused on the positive things in your life.

RESULTS OF PRAYER

After I shattered my elbow, rehab was brutal for me. An elbow joint replacement program takes approximately twelve weeks from surgery all the way to full recovery. Plus, if you don't work hard and exercise through all of the motions, your movement might never come back. When I first began, I wasn't off to a great start. Moving my arm after surgery was excruciating. I had to constantly remind myself: mind over matter. The doctor was telling me I could do it, but mentally I felt like I was defeated. I was very close to accepting that I would never be able move my arm.

I dreaded going to physical therapy, but I had a therapist who took the time to be a friend and supported me during my rehabilitation. I recall running out of sessions covered by my insurance and my insurance not covering specific machines to use in rehab, but she did not let that stop her. She did everything in her power to help me get my arm moving again. I remember one session where I felt like giving up. Depression had sunk in, and I thought that I would never be able to pick up my daughter again. There were tears in my eyes, but I couldn't let them fall. I was still holding on to my faith.

That triggered something within me. My physical therapist reminded me that I had a purpose.

She knew that I had broken more than just my elbow. She knew that if this was going to work, she had to help me repair my mind first. She worked to turn my negative self-talk into positive. She looked at me and asked me, "Why do you want your motion back? What is it that motivates you for a full recovery? Is that reason strong enough to push through this pain?"

In that moment she triggered something within me. She reminded me that I did have a purpose. And by the grace of God and her support I was able to begin moving my elbow again in less than five months.

My insurance only covered three months of rehab, but I received more than five months of assistance. God was answering my prayers. The cost was the same! God heard my prayers to accept his power for healing, and he made it possible. The miracle did not come exactly the way I imagined, but it happened.

Also, during this time, I was blessed to have a boss that allowed me to work with my broken arm. I only missed two days of work. My emergency fund of $1,000 was smoked instantly back in June. I did not get my surgery until the 4th of July. I even had a co-worker come pick me up and help me get in and out of cars even though I shouldn't have been working at that time. God knew I needed the money to help provide for my family.

Some might call this a coincidence, but it was because of prayer. I had the best surgeon perform my surgery, a physical therapist who went the extra mile to help me regain motion, a compassionate manager who let me earn money even when I wasn't physically at 100 percent, and a generous co-worker who took care of me for months. Every problem that I thought was too big, God solved it by moving parts I did not know could work in my favor.

PRAYER IS YOUR ENERGY SOURCE.
Persistence will drain you. The more you consistently do, the more tired you will get, which is why it's essential to stay connected to the source. God will be there to remind you that you are incapable of fatigue when he is the source of your motivation. Who better to remind you of your strength than the provider?

Paying off debt and managing day to day financial obligations is mentally taxing. Prayer allows time for you to relax your mind. Take a regular UFC mixed martial arts match for example. In a UFC fight, two fighters go toe to toe in an octagon ring. Every punch, kick, and takedown move they make takes effort and causes damage to their opponents. After each round, fighters go back to their respective corners and take a breather. They get a place to sit for a second, a moment to take rest, and have some water. Trainers take time to put them at ease and give them a burst of motivation to finish the next round. Fighters win by putting everything they have into the ring, round after round.

Prayer is your rest, reset, and get-ready-again time during your financial journey—it will get you prepared to get up for another round. Pray with intention and focus on the purpose. During my prayer time I find my peace. Sometimes I even receive inspiration.

Mental Wealth is a product of prayer.

Take the time and be intentional about your recharge. You will be amazed at what will happen. Before life beats you up and pushes you to the brink pray and get ready for the next round.

MY PRAYER FOR YOU
Dear God,

Father, I thank you for your love, peace, and abundance. I pray that this book, and specifically this chapter, opens the communication channel back to you as we surrender to your omnipotent good. We are ready to become better expressions of our divinity. We embrace your abundant nature. We embrace our great health. We are resting spiritually in your peace. We are becoming mentally stronger with every problem you ordain us to solve. We understand that we are here to share your love with our brother, our sisters, and all your creations, whom we share this experience with. We are receptive to the opportunities, wisdom, and inspiration you provide as we welcome more of your abundance into our lives. We know that we cannot do this alone, so we ask for guidance. From this day forth, our minds are changed, as we obtain Mental Wealth.

Amen.

CONCLUSION

—

PASSING THE BUCK

Money is not the root of all evil, and we must break free from the lies we hear about money being this wicked thing. It is a good thing, but it must be adequately managed and is intended to serve you. Your money is useful if you are knowledgeable. You can change multiple generations by how you handle every dollar you touch.

We've already gone over the five Ps of Mental Wealth, but why do they matter? I want you to think about the questions below and what you want to do with your life. Eliminating debt gives you options, and those options help you decide how to build wealth while creating an immortal legacy.

Do you have someone you care for?

Do you want to do something special for them?

If you had your life to live over again, would you do things differently?

THE FUNERAL

It was a cold rainy day, but I promised my co-worker I would be at her dad's funeral. I have been to several funerals in my lifetime, so I knew what to expect. I was prepared to see people cry and talk about how they would truly miss the person that had passed. This funeral was unique because it was for a Burmese family. I was the only black person there. The entire funeral was also conducted in their native language of Burmese. To be honest I went out of respect, but even before I got there, I knew it would be different.

There were literally over five hundred people in attendance. So many people were at this man's funeral that I remember thinking he must have been famous. But fame had nothing to with why so many people arrived to celebrate this man's life. I was blessed to have another co-worker sit next to me, and she translated the entire funeral to me.

My heart was touched by all the remarks they made about this man. Coming to America was a significant achievement for him, and he never wasted a second of his life. There were waves of tears and sadness in the room. His daughter shared stories about how her father helped people in the community learn how to drive, paid for all his children to complete school, and even transported people back and forth to the hospital.

Although stomach cancer took his life, he lived a prosperous life. He impacted everyone that came to the funeral, particularly his family. My co-worker's father left no debt behind, there was peace made with everyone in his household, and he even gifted his children a bible. In each bible, he marked his favorite bible verse, inspiring their walk with God. I have no clue about his net worth at the time of his funeral, but I know he died rich. He was rich in love, charity, and peace.

This moment was special to me, and it caused me to reflect on what wealth is.

Money is significant, but it is not the end all be all.

We need it to take care of ourselves and fund our dreams to impact the world. Hoarding piles of cash or living a life full of envy is not beneficial. We are here today and gone tomorrow. Life is delicate, and our time here is only temporary. What will the relics of your life be?

We spend so much of our time wandering this earth mostly lost. Many of us never find our way. We work jobs that will replace us in twenty-four hours. We allow ourselves to get lost in the standard patterns of life. Along the way, we forget what makes life worth living. The love of family, the joy of charity, and the peace of fulfilling God's will for personal happiness make life worth living.

Stop living a life that feels like death is dancing at your heels. Begin to implement the qualities of life that make the dance of life more meaningful. Take time for yourself. Spend your extra time giving to those who temporarily have less. You do not have to be financially well off to make a difference. Time is so precious. Don't be willing to exchange most of your time on earth working just to pay bills. We are always on borrowed time.

It is a blessing to experience life. Share your joy, and you will spend your life sharing God's will. Death is inevitable. Science can extend our longevity and we can freeze our bodies, but eventually our number will be called. When God calls your name, what will the memories of your life be?

WHAT WILL YOUR LEGACY BE?

Failure to reach financial freedom in your lifetime will burden your children. Mental Wealth was written with the following objectives in mind:

1. Healthy financial mindsets help create better overall mindsets, which leads to financial freedom.
2. Real wealth is more than money; however, financial wealth takes strategy and innovation to achieve first because it opens so many doors.
3. Wealth is a holistic combination of finances, relationships, health, mental wellness, and spiritual alignment.

These three lessons can all be unlocked with knowing your purpose, creating an achievable plan, surrounding yourself with the right people, going through life with perseverance, and praying with a grateful heart.

Your purpose brings meaning to your journey and sparks the fuel necessary to accomplish everything. It is hard to believe in something if your heart is not in it. There may have been things in your life that have impacted the way you view yourself, but that mindset can change when you know your purpose.

Without a plan, you will experience failure. You must have a winning mindset and be motivated to take action to get there. The Bible states, "faith without works is dead," James 2:26. Proverbs 16:9 states, "In their hearts, humans plan their course, but the Lord establishes their steps." Get serious and create a wealth plan for your family—not just a budget. Starting with a budget is okay, but I want you to plan more prominent than the finite, plan for the infinite.

We were created to share in God's abundance. Relationships are vital for your success.

People will help you or hold you back. It is up to you on who should be a part of your journey. There are no awards for finishing this race by yourself so you should get good at picking who is on your team. The most successful people have teams. Your mindset about people needs to reflect your values and move you closer to life goals.

Do not give up when times are rough. COVID-19 has struck the world and changed how we do life, but that should not change the mindset you have toward becoming debt-free and building wealth for your family in the years to come. So, embrace the trials and let them make you stronger. Remember your "why" and stay focused on the task at hand.

Prayer will keep you charged up on what direction to go in. I cannot stress enough the importance of this part of the process. Prayer will remind you that your life is more significant than the money you accumulate. No amount of money will make you feel secure if you are not fulfilling God's will in your life. Practice gratitude and have faith that God has you on the way to financial freedom.

This entire process taught you principles to apply to your money. You are stealing from others you care about when you do not think about the effects of all your financial decisions today. Your journey to financial freedom will be unique to who you are. Though we may all battle and struggle with similar issues. These issues bring unnecessary stress. The process of correcting them is different for all of us. Developing Mental Wealth will turn your hard work into a blessing for generations to come.

We cannot take anything with us, but we can leave something behind. The question is, what? When you are in debt and cannot see tomorrow because you are stuck in today it is hard for you to think about others. However, that challenge does not eliminate the need to think about them. Your descendants should be able to look back and remember how you set them up for success. How you set them up is up to you. Some people leave life insurance policies, family businesses, properties, or trust funds. It can be a mixture of all of these if you would like. The key is just to leave something of value.

The day I transition, I want people to remember me beyond my bank account. I want my family to know I was a man of integrity and a person who cared for them. Yes, I will leave them money, but I will also leave them the foundation that created wealth. This book was written to last from generation to generation, principles to change their lives and their finances. However, this book is just not for my family. It is for yours too. I want you to leave a legacy worth remembering. A healthy mindset is your greatest asset.

ACKNOWLEDGMENTS

First and foremost, I want to thank God for giving me the vision and ability to complete this book.

Mental Wealth was a dream that everyone made possible through their support.

I want to give a special thank you to my wife Selam. You continuously allow me to pursue all my crazy ideas and support me through all the highs and lows of entrepreneurship. I would also like to show my gratitude to my children Samiyah, Noah, and Yuel for being an inspiration to me to live out my dreams, so they can see there are no limits to what's inside of them.

Mom and Grandma, thank you for seeing the potential in me as little kid and giving me the gift of learning and confidence to push toward unchartered waters.

Special thanks to the NDP and Georgetown team! I could not have done this without you. I am forever grateful for you all.

David, your friendship and help on this project was special. I hope I get an opportunity to return the favor!

Lastly to all my early supporters! Thank you for every post, comment, share, and purchase of Mental Wealth. The Movement has begun, and you are tuned in!

Aaron Laster	Charles Hicks
Aden Hagos	Cheryl Bentley
Adriana Guevara-Pina	Christian Golden
Al Riddick	Christian Wellmann
Alena Cowley	Cj Montgomery
Alexis Johnson	Colleen Ritchie
Amantha Lott	Cordaryl Taylor
Andrew Adeniyi	Corey Johnson
Angel Shenice Longino	Corina Sullivan
Angela Anderson	Dakota Tucker
Anthony M Smith	Daniel Joel Benefiel
Anthony Murdock II	Darius Parker
Asantua Williams	Dave Macon' Jr.
Ashley Patterson	Dayonna Lewis
Ben Slaughter	Dedric R. Dennist, Sr.
Bernard Mickle	DeNai Donaville
Bethsaida Consulting Group	Deona Williams
Bianca Wright	Diondria Brown
Bordoli Kiflai	Donna Kreps
Brian Johnson	Drew Dawson
Calik Reaves	Drew Parker
Calik Reaves	Eboni Wolfe
Carissa Sullivan	Elilta Tsegai
Casey Hicks	Elise Hunter
Casey Madsen	Emaelaf Alemu

Emanuel Sangster
Eric Koester
Filimon Adhanom
Fred Haley Sr
Haben Ghebremichael
Hanna Weber
Isaac Sanchez
Isaac Wooten
Isaiah Manriquez
J. Croom
Jacquelyn Opara
Jamar T. Williams
James Bigsbee
Jana Heidenreich
Jasmine Graves
Jason Talbert
Jeffery Vardiman
Jesse slaugh
Jessica Parks
Jim Gilkey
Jonathan Ember
Jonathan Tarver
Jordan McKinney
Jose Rivera
Joshua Walker
Kali Vaughn
Kathleen Sensing
Kathy Sherron-Higgins
Kelly Maxwell
Kevin Lott
Kevin StCyr
Kidan Asgedom

Kurnitra Hicks
Lamar Washington
London Borom
Marc Hardy
Maria Santiago
Mariah Broader
Marquez Carlisle
Marquis Peterson
Martin Angus Jr.
Mary Adeniyi
Mary Carter
Matt Robinson
Maxine Hill
Melvin L Evans
Merhawit Measho
Michael D. Clark
Michael Galford
Mignon Ramsey
Mike Pirtle
Moacir Feldenheimer
Momma Crib
Natasha Cheatham
Nikkia Jackson
Nyat Adhanom
Oraine Munda
Pauline Parker
Pete Edwards
Qaadir Purham
Raquel Davis
Raymond L Davis III
Renea Maxfield
Rick Allen

Robert B. Reed
Rodney Carpenter
Ryan Ligon
Samuel George
Samuel Reed lll
Sancheon White
Saron Berhe
Saundriese Rias
Schanelle McCall
Seimon Adhanom
Selam Adhanom
Sequoia Lee
Shante Patterson
Shauna Dickenson
Sheena Harris
Shervon Alvarez
Sinit Ghebrehiwet
Stacy Poindexter
Stephanie Y Velez
Stephen Bowman

Steven Thompson
Taishe Abrams
Tameca Reed
Tammy Reed
Terrance Harrell
Terri Sheppard
Tiara Mickle
Tonya Davis
Trevor Holloway
Tyiree Phillips
Tyler Kelley
Unique reed
Uzoma F. Obidike
Valentin Emmanuel
Victoire Iradukunda
Walter McDonald
William McLaurin
William Sanders
Yodit Alemu

APPENDIX

—. 2019.The Infinite Game.Portfolio/Penguin.

"Agape Spiritual Principles and Practices." AgapeLive. Accessed May 30, 2020. http://www.agapelive.com/pages/agape-spiritual-principles-and-practices.

"Alcohol and Debt - What Are the Problems & Effects." Creditfix, August 15, 2017. https://www.creditfix.co.uk/blog/alcohol-debt-problems-effects/.

Alcuff, John. 2017.Finish: Give Yourself the Gift of Done.Portfolio (September 12, 2017).

Ashe-Edmunds, Sam. "Importance of Keeping a Budget." budgeting.thenest.com. Accessed April 30, 2020. https://budgeting.thenest.com/importance-keeping-budget-20559.html.

BET Networks. "Robert F. Smith's Morehouse Student Loan Pledge Will Also Include Graduate's Parents." BET.com, September 20, 2019. https://www.bet.com/news/national/2019/09/20/robert-f--smith_s-morehouse-student-loan-pledge-will-also-includ.html.

BrainyMedia Inc. "Hal Borland Quotes." BrainyQuote, 2020.
https://www.brainyquote.com/quotes/hal_borland_143123.

Buehler, Roger, and Dale Griffin. "The Planning Fallacy: Cognitive,
Motivational, and Social Origins."Advances in Experimental
Social Psychology43 (2010): 1–62.

Carse, James P.Finite and Infinite Games : A Vision of Life as Play
and Possibility. 1986. New York: Free Press, n.d.

Daniel Mark Epstein.The Lincolns : Portrait of a Marriage. New
York: Ballantine Books, 2009.

Feuer, Susan.Believing in Ourselves : The Wisdom of Women.
Kansas City: Andrews Mcmeel Pub, 2001.

Goldsmith, Barton. "Money & Emotions." Psychology Today, 2018.
https://www.psychologytoday.com/us/blog/emotional-fit-
ness/201804/money-emotions.

Gordon, Jon.The Energy Bus : 10 Rules to Fuel Your Life, Work, and
Team with Positive Energy. Chichester, West Sussex: Wiley, 2015.

Groth, Aimee. "You're The Average Of The Five People You Spend
The Most Time With - Business Insider." Business Insider.
Business Insider, July 24, 2012. https://www.businessinsider.
com/jim-rohn-youre-the-average-of-the-five-people-you-
spend-the-most-time-with-2012-7.

Hall, Ryan. The EntreLeadership Podcast Episode 336: Run the
Mile You Are In. Interview by Alex Judd, August 18, 2019.

"How to Defeat Wishful Thinking." HCPLive®, 2016. https://www.mdmag.com/physicians-money-digest/contributor/future-proof-md/2016/12/how-to-defeat-wishful-thinking.

"How to Defeat Wishful Thinking." HCPLive®, December 29, 2016. https://www.mdmag.com/physicians-money-digest/contributor/future-proof-md/2016/12/how-to-defeat-wishful-thinking.

Joe Rogan. "Fear Factor," n.d.

"Kevin Gates on The Worst Money He's Ever Blown | Men's Wealth | Men's Health." YouTube Video.YouTube, November 21, 2019. https://www.youtube.com/watch?v=GL-SE7-UZTQ&feature=youtu.be.

Manes, Yvette. "5 Ways Toxic Friendships Could Be Hurting Your Health." Insider. Accessed April 30, 2020. https://www.insider.com/signs-of-a-bad-friendship-health-2018-5.

Martin, Emmie. "The Government Shutdown Spotlights a Bigger Issue: 78% of US Workers Live Paycheck to Paycheck." CNBC. CNBC, January 9, 2019. https://www.cnbc.com/2019/01/09/shutdown-highlights-that-4-in-5-us-workers-live-paycheck-to-paycheck.html.

Munroe, Myles. "Dr Myles Munroe | The Purpose for Your Life." YouTube, May 8, 2017. https://youtu.be/EJ7Xz_mLsN4.

Nightingale, Earl.Earl Nightingale's Greatest Discovery : "The Strangest Secret-- Revisited."New York: Dodd, Mead, 1987.

O'Neal, Antony. "What No One Told You About Student Loans." The Borrowed Future Podcast, 20AD.

Perlman, Hope. "Carol Dweck's Mindset and a Yoga Mat Revelation." Psychology Today, 2012. https://www.psychologytoday. com/sg/blog/unmapped-country/201212/carol-dwecks-mindset-and-yoga-mat-revelation.

Ramsey, Dave. "Whats the Reason for the Debt Snowball - Ask Dave." daveramsey.com, 2020. https://www.daveramsey.com/ askdave/budgeting/whats-the-reason-for-the-debt-snowball.

Selig, Meg. "How Do Work Breaks Help Your Brain? 5 Surprising Answers." Psychology Today, 2018. https://www.psychologytoday.com/us/blog/changepower/201704/how-do-work-breaks-help-your-brain-5-surprising-answers.

"Silent and Solo: How Americans Pray." Barna Group, 2017. https://www.barna.com/research/silent-solo-americans-pray/.

Sinek, Simon. 2009.Start with The Why.Portfolio; Reprint edition (December 27, 2011).

Space Jam. Warner Bros. Pictures, n.d.

Student Loan Planner. "Student Loan Planner - Student Loan Advisor and Expert." Student Loan Planner, August 8, 2019. https://www.studentloanplanner.com/.

The Notorious B.I.G.Mo Money Mo Problems. Streamed, 1996.

The Notorious B.I.G. "The Notorious B.I.G. - Mo Money Mo Problems (Official Music Video)." YouTube Video.YouTube, 2020. https://www.youtube.com/watch?v=gUhRKVIjJtw.

"What No One Told You About Student Loans." daveramsey.com, 2019. https://www.daveramsey.com/blog/what-no-one-told-you-about-student-loans.

"Why Your Support System Is Important for Your Success." Herzing University, June 8, 2017. https://www.herzing.edu/blog/why-your-support-system-important-your-success.

Winfrey, Oprah. "Oprah's Gratitude Journal Oprah's Lifeclass Oprah Winfrey Network." YouTube Video.YouTube, October 26, 2013. https://www.youtube.com/watch?v=saZWjI-lwU8c&feature=youtu.be.

Zimbardo, Philip. 1971.The Stanrofd Prison Experiment.Research, Standford: Stanford University.